THE ROYAL GUIDE TO WAX FLOWER MODELLING • PEACHEY, EMMA

PAGE

Advantage of wax flower modelling over other fancy work 8 6
Anecdote—Bridal 32 13
Anemone Anemone Hortensis 20 9
Art of modelling wax flowers introduced into England 4 4
Awards of the press 61 21
Blossom 43 16
Botanical words, explanation of 13 7
Bouquets—her Majesty's marriage 32 13
Brushes, method of applying them 13 7
Brushes, how to cleanse 13 7
Cactus 53 19
Call for the book 1 3
Camellia, Variegated Variegata 50 ... 18
Carnation Dianthus 35 13
Chatsworth 58 20
Crocus Crocus Luteus 16 8
Crystal Palace 58 20
Curling pins and scissors, use of 12 7
Dahlia Dahlia 48 17
Daisy Bellis Perennis 23 10
Directions for mixing colours 11 6
Dry colouring, objections to 7 5
Exhibition, (Great) 58 20
Extract from family letters of his Grace the Duke of Devonshire 4 4
Foliage, Instructions for 56 19
Forget-me-not Myosotis 40 15
Flowers, mounting of, etc. 55 19
Flowers, various, to be described 15... 8
Floral life 15 8
Flowering seasons, the 15 8
Fuchsia Fuchsia Fulgens 38 14
Fuchsia, Crimson Fuchsia Coccinea 39 15
Geranium, Pink Pelargonium 40 15
Geranium, Scarlet 42 15
Grouping Flowers 54 19
Her Majesty's patronage 2 4
Hollyhock, Lemon Althæa 53 19
Honeysuckle Caprifolium 37 14
How to cleanse the scissors, pins, and marbles 13 7
Introduction 1 3
Jasmine, Yellow Jasminum Revolutum 28 11
Jasmine, White Jasminum Officinale 29 12
Jasmine, Cape Gardenia 29 12
Jonquil 23 10
Kalmia Kalmia Latifolia 28 11
[xvi]

Kew Gardens 8 6
Lilac Rhododendron 26 11
Lily, White Lilium Alba 44 16
Lily, Pink-spotted Lilium Lancifolium 45 16
Lily, White Water Nymphea Alba 46 17
Lily, Yellow Water Nymphea, Yellow 47 17
Lily, Blue Water Nymphea, Blue 47. 17
Materials required for wax flower modelling 8 6
Mignonette, (origin of) Reseda Odorata 42 15
Moral view of the art 4 4
Myrtle Myrtus Communis 36 14
Narcissus 23 10
Nature, how to copy from 14 7
Orange Blossom Citrus 43 16
Passion Flower Passiflora 51 18
Primrose Primula 17 8
Professional sketch, etc. 3 4
Progress of the art 5 5
Pupils—necessarily limited—testimony of former pupils 2 4
Purposes to which the materials are applied 9 6
Regent's Park Gardens 8 6
Rhododendron 26 11
Roses—instructions 30 12
Rose, Cabbage Rosa Centifolia 30.... 12
Rose, Moss Rosa Muscosa 32 13
Rose, White Rosa Alba 32 13
Rose, Damask Rosa Damascena 33 .. 13
Rose, Sweet-scented Tea Rosa Safrano 34 13
Rose, Yellow Rosa, Cloth of Gold 34 13
Rose, Austrian Briar Rosa Lutea 35.. 13
Salvia Salvia Patens 49 17
Seringa Oleineæ 44 16
Sir Joseph Paxton 58 20
Snowdrop Galanthus Nivalis 17 8
The *Lady's Newspaper*, articles in 2 ... 4
The Queen's warrant 3 4

The *Manchester Examiner* answered 65
The colours 10 6
Tulip, Van Thol Tulipa Præcox 22 ... 10
Tulip, Summer 22 10
Victoria Regia, The Victoria Regia 57 20
Violet, White Viola Odorata 19 9
Violet, Purple Viola Purpurea 20 9
Visitors 59 20
Wallflower Cheiranthus Cheiri 25 10
Wax Flowers, as ornaments for the hair 55 19
Wax, artistically prepared 6 5

Publisher's Note

Purchase of this book entitles you to a free trial membership in the publisher's book club at www.rarebooksclub.com. (Time limited offer.) Simply enter the barcode number from the back cover onto the membership form on our home page. The book club entitles you to select from millions of books at no additional charge. You can also download a digital copy of this and related books to read on the go. Simply enter the title or subject onto the search form to find them.

Note: This is an historic book. Pages numbers, where present in the text, refer to the first edition of the book and may also be in indexes.

If you have any questions, could you please be so kind as to consult our Frequently Asked Questions page at www.rarebooksclub.com/faqs.cfm? You are also welcome to contact us there.

Publisher: General Books LLC™, Memphis, TN, USA, 2012. ISBN: 9781153781244.

Proofreading: pgdp.net

✄ ✄ ✄ ✄ ✄ ✄ ✄ ✄

Front Cover
Back Cover

PEACHEY'S

ROYAL GUIDE

TO

WAX FLOWER MODELLING.

"God might have made the earth bring forth
Enough for great and small,
The oak tree and the cedar tree
Without a flower at all.

"Then wherefore, wherefore, were they made?
* * * * * *

"To comfort man—to whisper hope,
Whene'er his faith is dim;
For whoso careth for the flowers
Will much more care for Him ."

ADVERTISEMENT.

Mrs. Peachey being, for the reasons stated in this work, compelled to circumscribe the giving of lessons, if not to discontinue instructions altogether in a few months, the book will, therefore, under any circumstances, be indispensable.

J. Gardner & C. Zinc. 86 Hatton Garden.

THE
ROYAL GUIDE
TO
Wax Flower Modelling.
BY
MRS. PEACHEY,
Artiste to Her Majesty.

"For *not alone* to please the sense of *smell*,
Or charm the sight, are flowers to mankind given,—
A thousand sanctities do them invest,
And bright associations hallow them!
Which to the cultivated intellect
May give delight, and all the heart improve."

LONDON:

PUBLISHED AND SOLD BY MRS. PEACHEY,
ARTISTE TO HER MAJESTY,
AND SOLD BY ALL BOOKSELLERS.
MDCCCLI.
TO
THE PRINCESS ROYAL
OF
ENGLAND,
AS A TOKEN OF LOYAL AND GRATEFUL
ACKNOWLEDGEMENT
FOR THE SPONTANEOUS AND FOSTERING PATRONAGE OF HER ROYAL HIGHNESS'S AUGUST PARENT
THE QUEEN;
THE ROYAL GUIDE TO WAX FLOWER MODELLING
IS MOST RESPECTFULLY DEDICATED
BY HER ROYAL HIGHNESS'S MOST OBLIGED
AND OBEDIENT HUMBLE SERVANT,
EMMA PEACHEY,
ARTISTE TO HER MAJESTY.
[ix]

PREFACE.

The Editor of this work, by Her Majesty's Artiste, Mrs. Peachey , fairly entitled the Royal Guide to Wax Flower Modelling , would fain leave the introduction, written by the same hand which rivals nature in her varying adornments, to unfold its historic, its poetic, its moral, and its suggestive graces—for it combines these; but having accepted the part, without which, since the days of Plato, no book is deemed complete, he essays a few prefatory observations and remarks.

Brevity, it has been said, is the soul of wit; but we may be brief when we know what is to follow, and for whom the following pages are designed.

Our fair readers will intuitively perceive that the scope of the instructive portion of this self-commending [x] little volume is to facilitate their acquisition of an accomplishment at once royal and feminine in its origin and progress, and therefore worthy of their attention.

This elegant art requires but the fairy touch of a delicate hand to fill each available space in the chamber or drawing-room with the most perfect and beautiful imitations of the flower-garden.

"The morning flowers display their sweets,
And gay their silken leaves unfold,
As careless of the noontide heats,
As fearless of the winter cold.
"Nipped by the wind's unkindly blast,
Parched by the sun's directer ray,
The momentary glories waste,
The short-lived beauties die away."

Unaffected by change or climate, wax flower modelling perpetuates the transient glories of the floral seasons; places all the tender varieties under the immediate glance of the ever gratified eye of the artist, who can thus in the depth of winter exhibit to an admiring foreign guest the exotics of the far hemisphere, or the indigenous plants of her own loved land. [xi]

Who that has watched by the side of an invalid mother, would not feel an exalted pleasure in creating around her the magical representations of those flowerets and rosebuds her maternal hand was wont to rear? Who, in such a moment of ministering affection, would not feel how sweet the reward of a father's love, as his approving gaze spoke more than many words his thanks to the duteous child returning the early care of the fond partner of his griefs and joys? Contemplating such a scene as this, one cannot refrain from citing the language of the poet:—
"O! if there be a tear,
From passion's dross refined and clear;
A tear so limpid and so meek,
It would not stain an angel's cheek;
'Tis that which pious fathers shed
Upon a duteous daughter's head."

The copious table of contents possesses great attraction for persons of refined taste, embracing every variety of flower usually modelled in wax: its arrangement is calculated to lead the learner, by easy steps, from the most simple to the most elaborate accomplishment of a very delightful task. [xii]

The sketch of her artistic life, with which the talented though unpretending authoress has favoured the public, cannot fail to prove useful and encouraging to the beginner, as it fully justifies the good old proverb, that "where there is a will, there is a way;" and that way is clearly and forcibly pointed out in the Royal Guide , so as to direct with perfect ease the willing fingers of the modeller to the attainment of her object, to excel in giving form and substance to her innate perceptions of the beautiful. Nor is this a selfish pleasure. These productions of skilled labour—if we may apply the word labour to an amusement—please the beholder, as they do the mind which calls forth the exquisite fancy which pencils these flowers.

The unanimous verdict of the Press will be found recorded at the end of the instructions. It is a remarkable fact, that so many Journals, giving in their separate awards, should have all concurred in opinion. This opinion is highly favourable to the Artiste and the art. The very language in which it is couched partakes of floweriness—if we may be pardoned for coining [xiii] a word to express our meaning; indeed, we strongly commend for perusal these elegant notices of the Press; the writers evidently have been influenced by national considerations; for they speak of what they have seen as those convinced that, although there may be several wax flower modellers, there is but one Mrs. Peachey —Her Majesty's Artiste, and an Englishwoman.

It is with no insular feeling that we express the same sentiment; but, nevertheless, we do feel it to be something to boast of, that our countrywomen will not have to learn the art of Wax Flower Modelling from foreigners, many of whom however have been amongst the now nearly 50,000 visitors attracted to the collection, by the notices of the Press, and who have expressed equal approbation.

The Royal Guide is essentially a domestic national instructor. But its teaching will not be bounded by our island shores. We venture to predict, that the Royal Guide to Wax Flower Modelling will, ere long, establish for itself a more than European fame. [xiv]

The Editor would now conclude the task he has undertaken, and performed, as well as more immediate professional calls upon his time would permit, to the best of his abilities; but, beyond changing or transposing a word or term here and there, introducing some poetic gems, and correcting the press, he does not claim any merit for the work from his hands, that properly belongs to the Authoress, who has been called into the field, and to whom the reader is now fairly introduced, as to a pleasing and accomplished instructress in this Art. [xv]

[1]

PEACHEY'S ROYAL GUIDE

TO

WAX FLOWER MODELLING.

Before I commence my course of instruction in the fascinating art of representing in wax the floral beauties of nature, I deem it necessary to prelude by a brief explanation as to my pretensions, and the cause of my offering such instructions to the notice of the public.

I have constantly applied myself, during the last fourteen years, in strictly copying from nature every flower that has come under my notice, from the simple wild flowers of our hallowed native fields, to the latest and rarest exotics brought home by our most eminent collectors. I have also been materially assisted in this particular branch of my art, by the nobility and gentry having kindly granted me the indulgence of selecting as copies, from their conservatories, aught that I might consider as valuable additions to my specimens.

I have been frequently asked by my pupils to publish such a work as the present; but diffidence, amounting perhaps to a [2] weakness, has hitherto prevented me from even momentarily exchanging the pencil of the artist for the pen of the author:

"Authors, you know, of greatest fame,
Through modesty, suppress their name."

In the year 1847, I wrote several articles for the *Lady's Newspaper*, in the shape of instruction in Wax Flower Modelling, which articles appeared under the initials of "E. H., late pupil of Mrs. Peachey." I must confess I felt much gratified upon hearing my pupils, as well as other ladies, speak of these articles in terms of commendation. I trust I may be pardoned for this little piece of deception, and beg to remind those who might regard the "ingenious device" with censure, that Sir Walter Scott and many other writers of celebrity have done the same. If great and talented persons shrink from making their compositions known as their own creations, it is not surprising that I, who have no pretension to literature, should be equally tenacious of my incognito.

I have at this period determined upon publishing a book of instructions, purely in consequence of feeling quite inadequate to receive, as pupils, the numerous applicants that daily visit me, and express much anxiety to be initiated into my method of modelling and grouping.

They are two distinct things—to accomplish an art well, and to impart it to others. I hope I may not be considered egotistical in boldly asserting that, as an instructress, I stand pre-eminent. I feel proud, most proud, in having received repeated assurances from the distinguished and numerous ladies who have placed themselves under my tuition, that my method of teaching is such as to enable the most inexperienced to acquire with facility a perfect knowledge of this pleasing art.

The distinguished patronage I have from the first received at the hands of her Most Gracious Majesty, must surely convey to the minds of all, that I have a right to lay claim to artistic skill. [3]

When I first commenced the agreeable occupation of imitating nature, I had not the slightest idea of ultimately making it a profession. My anxious desire, I may say, my ambition, was to produce something that might be considered worthy the notice of our most Gracious Queen, who at the period I allude to, 1837, had just ascended the throne.

A spirit of loyalty had been fostered in me from my earliest infancy; and a pardonable glow of pleasure always animates me, at the remembrance that I am the daughter of an old officer, who served as surgeon in the British army the long period of fifty years. The result of my wishes has been great success. Our beloved Sovereign, ever ready to encourage talent or industry in any form, condescended to permit a bouquet, which I designed and executed for her inspection (in token of my loyalty), to be placed as an ornament in one of the royal palaces. This was indeed an honour I had scarcely dared to anticipate. Two years after the period alluded to, the Queen became acquainted with the fact, that a change of circumstances had compelled me to make the art of wax flower modelling a source of profit. Her Majesty, unsolicited by any, spoke to the then Lord Chamberlain relative to a warrant of appointment being granted to me; and I forthwith received the Royal Letters Patent, being the first in this country who enjoyed the privilege of being styled "Artist in Wax Flowers to Her Majesty." I hope I may not be deemed prolix in giving these particulars; it is not from any feeling of vanity, but from gratitude due to the high power that encouraged my talent in its infancy. The auspicious patronage I received gave an impetus to my labours; and I have from that royal day taxed my energies to the utmost, to prove that my works deserved the high honour that had been conferred upon them.

As this work is intended for the perusal of the young, as well as the adult, I trust I may be pardoned for pausing a [4] moment to dwell upon the all-wise dispensations of Providence. The talent which inspired me would have been useless, had not the "Giver of all good" discovered to me the knowledge that I possessed it; and I wish to impress upon the notice of my young friends and pupils, the advantage, I may say necessity, of embracing every opportunity of improving any talent committed to their charge; for my life has shown that what is acquired as an accomplishment or amusement, may one day become of vital importance to them.

It occurs to me, that it may not be uninteresting to many of my readers, to become acquainted with the period and by whom

THE ART OF MODELLING FLOWERS IN WAX WAS BROUGHT INTO ENGLAND.

I consequently subjoin an extract from Miss Strickland's Life of Mary Beatrice, second consort of James II., A.D. 1686.

"The beautiful imitations of natural flowers in wax which have lately afforded an attractive exercise for the taste and ingenuity of many of our youthful countrywomen, were first introduced into England by the mother of Mary Beatrice, as a present to her royal daughter; as we find by the following passage in a contemporary letter from a correspondent of the Lady Margaret Russell, which gives some information relative to the ornamental works then in vogue among ladies of rank, in the court of Mary Beatrice.

"'In gum flowers, Mrs. Booth tells me you and she is to doe something in that work, which I suppose must be extraordinary. I hope it will be as great perfection as the fine WAX WORK ye queen has, of nun's work, of fruit and flowers, that her mother did put up for her, and now she has 'em both for her chapel and her rooms. I do not know whether they be the four seasons of the year, but they say they are done so well, that they that see 'em can hardly think 'em other than the real.'" [A]

[A] In the collection of private family letters of the Duke of Devonshire, at Chiswick Lodge: copied by courteous permission of his Grace. [5]

From the year last named until 1736 I have been unable to trace any knowledge of this elegant art.

When wax flowers were again introduced by an Italian, they were clumsily manufactured in comparison to those seen in the present age of improvement; for I had the opportunity of inspecting some of their "miserable remains" but a few years since. Still I must acknowledge I discovered some taste and much ingenuity in their construction, and am not too proud to own that I benefited even by examining these very inferior productions. I feel quite satisfied that the art of wax flower modelling is almost still in its infancy. It is no longer regarded as an amusement only. It is enumerated with other accomplishments essential to female education. It assists botanical studies, and promotes the views of flower painters, either in oil or water colours; even in drawing, wax flowers will be found excellent auxiliaries, far preferable as copies to the even surface of plates. I have myself been much gratified by furnishing flowers in wax to some of our first flower painters, who have assured me that they have proved of great utility, in cases where the evanescent properties of the flower of nature prevented the possibility of committing their similitude to canvas ere their beauty had faded. It affords me no small degree of satisfaction also, that my flowers were found useful as copies for some of the beautiful carved work in the late great and ever memorable Exhibition. I have also supplied them as illustrations to botanical lectures.

In thus referring to the utility of wax flowers, I am reminded of a partially unfavourable prejudice which has lately sprung up, from an article which first appeared in a Manchester paper, and which was subsequently copied into *The Times*, and other papers. It is possible ladies may be induced to abandon this delightful amusement, upon reading such a statement as the subjoined extract: [6] —

" The Danger of Modelling in Wax. — Few persons, especially, perhaps, of the many young ladies who are now practising the very pleasing art of modelling fruits, flowers, &c., in wax, at all suspect the great danger in which they are placed from the poisonous nature of the colouring matter of the wax which they handle so unsuspectingly. The white wax, for instance, contains white lead; the green, copper; the yellow, chrome yellow and vermilion—strong poisons all; while many other kinds of wax are equally poisonous, and, therefore dangerous. There are very many persons who are aware of the intense sufferings, for very many years past, of Mr. W. Bally, phrenologist and modeller in wax, in which latter branch he has laboured for 24 or 25 years, three of them as teacher of the art, at the Manchester Mechanics' Institution. Mr. Bally has been at times completely paralysed, and is now and has long been very nearly so, especially in the hands and arms; and he has also been afflicted with extensive ulceration of the throat, and has almost totally lost his voice. Both himself and his medical adviser, after a long attention to his symptoms, are satisfied that the primary cause of his affliction is the extent to which the subtle poisons in the wax with which he has worked have been absorbed into his system through the pores of his hands, while the disease has been generally strengthened, and one part of it accounted for, by the occasional application of his fingers to his lips while at work. Mr. Bally says, that he has known several cases in which young ladies have been attacked with partial paralysis of the hands and arms, after having devoted some time to the practice of modelling; but at the time he had no suspicion of the cause. As all the requisite colours can be obtained from vegetable matter, and as the use of mineral colouring seems to lead to such deplorable results, the subject should be carefully investigated by those working with coloured wax."—*Manchester Examiner.*

It is not my intention to contradict an assertion so boldly set forth. I have no doubt the editor of the *Manchester Examiner* had some grounds for the article; but I think it right to state *that* which I can prove—namely, that the wax *artistically manufactured by me* is so perfectly harmless, that for the last fourteen years I have had it in my hands, upon an average from twelve to fourteen hours every day (Sunday excepted), and never in the slightest degree experienced any inconvenience or ill effects.

The small portion of colour I introduce undergoes a [7] chemical process, which neutralizes entirely any deleterious properties appertaining to the few colours required to be used. It is quite unnecessary to introduce white lead at all. I was assisted by a practical German chemist to prepare borax, in such a manner, as to entirely supersede white lead. Now most of my readers will be able to testify how perfectly harmless must be borax, it being one of the drugs so constantly used with honey, and recommended by the faculty as an excellent remedy for canker in the mouth. I am, as I have previously stated, the daughter of a medical man, and am perfectly acquainted with the danger attending the absorption of mineral colours into the system: under these circumstances, it is not likely that I should myself use that which would be injurious. Ladies, who desire to enjoy the recreation of wax flower modelling, may indulge in the amusement with perfect safety, if they purchase the wax of me. At the same time, I wish it to be perfectly understood, that I do not insinuate, or attribute aught against any other person or persons who prepare wax for sale.

I DECIDEDLY OBJECT to the dry colours being rubbed into the wax with the fingers. I invariably apply the colours with a brush. It must be injurious to close the pores of the skin, even were the powders so used innocuous; but to say nothing of the danger of the method alluded to, it is a most dirty occupation, and ladies would not like to see their hands dyed with carmine, Prussian blue, or chromes. Such a method of tinting is likely to prejudice ladies against the work altogether; besides which, it renders the flowers much more fragile. The only time I ever use dry powder is in the form of bloom (peculiarly prepared arrowroot), which I throw on lightly, but never rub in. Having endeavoured to prove that there are no dangerous results likely to accrue from this pleasing occupation, I will proceed to shew [8]

THE ADVANTAGE OF WAX MODELLING, OVER OTHER FANCY WORK.

And one great consideration is that the sight is not likely to be injured. The eye does not require to be fixed; it does not occupy so much attention as to prevent conversation, nor need the *body be bent*,—a matter of much importance with growing girls, many having suffered affections of the chest, and others disfigured for life, through continually stooping to frame work.

There is no monotony in this agreeable employment, for new varieties are continually springing up in nature; and a visit to the Botanical Gardens at Kew, or the Regent's Park, will at all seasons afford some fresh specimen. In referring to the former gardens, I cannot forbear expressing the deep sense of obligation I feel due from the public, and artists particularly—being myself one of them,—for the boon bestowed upon us by those powers who afford such facility for inspecting—free of charge—all that is lovely, choice, and rare. It is perfectly clear, according to my method, that the most elegant drawing room might be used, without suffering in its appearance during its operations. I would merely recommend that the table should be covered with paper, so that all small pieces might be kept together, and easily removed.

I will now proceed to name the

MATERIALS REQUIRED FOR WAX FLOWER MODELLING.

Wax —white, yellow, orange, pink, and several shades of green.

Two steel pins with china heads (different sizes). [9]

One ivory pin, with large head.

Eleven bottles of powder; consisting of scarlet, bright crimson, dark crimson, lemon, yellow, orange, dark orange, light blue, middle blue, dark blue, and white.

Twelve large brushes.
Two small brushes.
Twelve saucers.
Three skeins of white wire.
Two skeins of green do.
Two pieces of white marble, 3 to 4 inches square, ¾ inch thick.
One pair of sharp pointed scissors.
One cake of smalt.
One cake of sepia.
One cake of crimson lake.
One bottle of down.

Having given a list of the materials required for the elegant and charming amusement of "Wax Flower Modelling," I deem it expedient to make a few remarks relative to the properties of, and

PURPOSES TO WHICH THE MATERIALS ARE APPLIED.

Without wishing to derogate from the merit of others, or retaining to myself the exclusive ability of vending the purest wax and the best of other articles to be used in obtaining a faithful representation of nature, I think it necessary to state, that I offer to the public materials only of the very best quality; consequently, I take the prices of other persons' goods as no criterion or standard for mine. The wax is manufactured under my own immediate superintendence; soft, and perfectly dull on one side. It is sufficiently opaque [10] of itself not to require being painted on the wrong side for white flowers, which is the case with common wax. I likewise prepare wax, called "double wax," it is twice as thick as the ordinary wax. When the single wax is used double, the two shining sides should be placed together. It has sheets of tissue paper placed between it to keep each sheet of wax smooth and straight (a great advantage,) for when this is not done (though the wax may be good), the edges are often wrinkled, and a great deal of waste is the consequence.

The Colours —eleven in number, submitted for sale on my counters, 160, 161, 162, 163, Soho Bazaar, are of the very best quality, and ground down particularly fine in spirits. I recommend saucers instead of a flat pallet, as it is not necessary to use up at once all the colour that is mixed; and by keeping each colour distinct in separate saucers, much waste is prevented.

Twelve brushes are indispensable; each to be confined to the use of one colour. Two small sable brushes are for veining, as in geraniums.

The large ivory pin is required for the Victoria Regia, water-lily, and other large flowers.

The two smaller pins are to be used for similar purposes, on flowers of less magnitude.

The cake colours are never to be used alone, but rubbed down with the powder, as will be shown in my instructions for mixing colours.

The large white wire is to be used as stems for flowers, such as dahlia, camellia, &c.

The second and finest white wire to support the petals.

The green wire, Nos. 1 and 2, are for stems of various flowers.

The square pieces of marble are of great utility in rolling fine filaments, or rays, for the various kinds of passion flowers. [11] It is a much quicker and cleaner method than rolling them with the fingers.

I think it necessary to give some

DIRECTIONS FOR MIXING COLOURS.

Place the powder required in a saucer: add a few drops of water, and rub the same with a brush for some time; as friction materially improves the brilliancy of tint. The colour should be mixed as thick as cream, but a very small portion taken into the brush at one time. As the brushes are large, they absorb a large quantity of colour; consequently, the brush used to mix the colour with, must be pressed upon the edge of the saucer several times to cleanse it.

The cake paint is used with the powder colours for fine veining, and when a second colour is required to be placed over another; as I shall show in my instruction for the rich dahlia purpurea. I have a great objection to mixing gum water with the colours. I use it only previous to throwing on down, such as in the calyx of geranium, primrose, &c.

A rich crimson is produced by the application of the crimson powder upon pink wax.

A darker crimson, by adding a little of the darkest crimson powder to the former. If a deeper crimson still be required, add a little of the middle blue.

A pale pink is obtained by applying crimson powder with a small portion of white, laid on the wax very thin.

A light orange scarlet, as in fuchsia fulgens, is acquired by mixing a minute portion of scarlet powder with the bright crimson.

Scarlet for geranium; a larger portion of the scarlet with the crimson.

Different shades of scarlet are also produced by laying [12] the crimson powder upon different shades of wax, namely, lemon, yellow, and orange.

A purple (as in violet), is produced by mixing the second blue with a lesser portion of the bright crimson powder.

A deeper purple, as in the centre of the anemone, is obtained by the combination of the crimson powder with the deepest blue.

Various shades of lilac and peach colours are produced by a careful admixture of the bright crimson, middle blue, and white.

A primrose colour is obtained by using my lemon powder (a beautiful preparation), upon white wax.

A rich brown, as in wall-flower, requires a mixture of cake sepia with bright crimson.

The dark velvet-purple-looking spot seen in geraniums is obtained from mixing the cake smalt with a little bright crimson powder.

A similar tint may be obtained by mixing crimson lake, in cake, with the middle blue.

Various shades of green are procured by combining the first or second yellow with the darkest blue.

In noticing the

USE OF CURLING PINS AND SCISSORS,

I beg to remind my readers that these are the only instruments I deem requisite for modelling wax flowers. Both these require to be moistened before they are applied to the wax. Warmth as well as moisture is essential for these. A glass of lukewarm water will answer the purpose; but great care must be taken to shake off the surplus water; for if the globules were to fall upon the petal, it would occasion the colour to run.

[13]

THE METHOD OF APPLYING BRUSHES

requires to be stated; for they must not be held as a pen or pencil, but perfectly perpendicular. Commence a short distance from the lower end of the petals—for where the paint is applied the wax will not adhere. When the petal is all one colour, pass the brush from you quickly and lightly off the same on to the paper. If it is a variegated petal, bring the brush towards you. This will enable you to soften off the edges of the spots which are to be left free from colour. When moisture is required in the brush, the latter must not be plunged into water, but a small drop taken up by the handle on to the paper.

TO CLEANSE THE SCISSORS, PINS, AND MARBLES.

Dip either into boiling water, and wipe them immediately. The marbles require to be used warm.

EXPLANATION OF BOTANICAL WORDS.

Although I do not pretend to put this forth as a "Botanical work," I deem it necessary that I should make use of certain words in application to forming the different parts of a flower; I shall give an explanation of such botanical words as I must occasionally make use of in the course of my instructions.

Corolla signifies a flower deprived of its centre. For example: the corolla of a rhododendron falls from its position, leaving the interior of the flower pendent to the stem. The convolvulus has a funnel-shaped corolla.

Petal. This is part of the corolla, and what is termed, by the uninformed—leaf; for instance, we hear of drying rose leaves, when in fact it is the petals that are alluded to. The term leaf should only be applied to the foliage. [14]

Pistil , or Pistillum , is that part of a flower which projects directly from the centre, and is longer than the rest; we observe it in the white lily, fuchsia, honeysuckle, etc. The enlargement at the end of the pistil is termed stigma.

Stamens , or Stamina , signify the filaments that surround the pistil; and the enlarged part at the end of each filament is called anther.

Farina is the fine dust which is contained in the anther, and which shows itself also outside.

Calyx is applied to the green attached to the flower. For example: the part that is covered with moss about the rose is the calyx. Sometimes the calyx is covered with down, as in geranium, primrose, etc.

Stigma. The enlargement at the end of the pistillum.

HOW TO COPY FROM NATURE.

To take the pattern of a natural flower, you must remove the petals carefully, sorting out how many there are of an equal size. Take the shape of one out of each set, in the following manner: Place the petal upon a sheet of writing paper, holding it firmly to the paper with the point of the fore finger of the left hand. Take a large brush containing a very little colour and pass it round the edge. The exact form will be left upon the paper without tearing the edges of the petal, even though it were unusually fragile. When the requisite flower cannot be procured, a proper pattern can be obtained at Soho Bazaar, or at my residence, 35, Rathbone Place, where I am happy to receive visitors, daily, from ten in the morning till six o'clock in the evening. Place the pattern upon the dull side of the wax, and as the grain runs the length of the same, cut each petal accordingly, for the wax takes the paint much better in that direction.

[15]

VARIOUS FLOWERS TO BE DESCRIBED.

FLORAL LIFE.

"Lord, what is life? 'Tis like a flower
That blossoms, and is gone!
We see it flourish for an hour,
With all its beauty on;
But death comes, like a wintry day,
And cuts the pretty flower away."

THE FLOWERING SEASONS.

"Say, what impels, amid surrounding snow
Congealed, the Crocus' flowery bud to glow?
Say, what retards, amid the summer blaze,
The autumnal bud, till pale declining days?
"The God of seasons, whose pervading power
Controls the sun, or sheds the fleecy shower;
He bids each flower His quickening word obey,
Or to each lingering bloom enjoins delay."
H. Kirke White.

As it will be impossible in a small volume to give instructions in all Flowers, I shall endeavour to select such as will produce a pleasing contrast of form and colour; at the same time, including flowers of every season, commencing with Spring—and who does not hail the early Flowers with delight? After a long and severe winter, the appearance of the golden crocus and the modest snowdrop, peeping from the earth, convey to the mind a glow of unspeakable pleasure.

"Then wherefore had they birth?
To minister delight to man—
To beautify the earth."

[16]

INSTRUCTION HOW TO FORM THE CROCUS.

(Crocus Luteus.) *Youthfulness.*

Prepare the petals (from pattern) in double wax, choosing a bright orange, but not too dark. Place the two shining sides of the wax together. The inner petals are not striped, but the three outer ones have eight or ten pencil strokes of a middle shade of green, broad towards the lower end, and carried off to fine points; these strokes do not extend beyond two thirds of the flower, and laid on with the sable brush. Cup the petals very much with a large head pin (this is why they require to be cut from double wax) so firmly that each petal produces an egg-shaped form when united. Double a hem in a piece of wax the same as that from which you have previously cut the petals. Prepare the stamina from this piece of wax by snipping the proper number. The hem at the edge of the wax is to represent the anthers; affix the stamina when so prepared to the end of a piece of strong wire, and cover them with farina (my second yellow powder). Place the petals round the stamina—first, the three not painted—and the remaining three in the intervening spaces.

The calyx is prepared in lemon wax, tinged with a little brown, and is passed round the end of the flower. The stem covered with pale lemon wax. The leaves narrow strips of double wax (dark green), strongly indented with the point of the pin, and a white stripe laid smoothly on with the small sable brush.

The above directions will answer for the crocus susianus, the cloth of gold, striped orange, and very dark purple; besides the Scotch crocus, striped, white, and purple.

[17]

THE SNOWDROP.

(Galanthus Nivalis.) *Consolation.*

"The snowdrop, and then the violet,
Arose from the ground with warm rain wet;
And their breath was mixed with fresh odour sent
From the turf, like the voice and the instrument."

This charming, pensive little flower should be prepared from double white wax. It consists of six petals, like its companion the crocus. The longest are left perfectly white, the others striped upon the inside with very light green paint; and upon the opposite or exterior side of the petal is placed a triangular green spot, near the off end. Cut a fine green wire, three inches long, cover it with a strip of light green wax, affix to the end the stamina, cut from yellow wax. Place round these the striped petals, and those that are quite white immediately between; finish off the same by placing a little double green wax at the end of the flower, which forms the calyx; the flower-stalk is then to be attached to a stronger stem. Where they are united place a small sheath, cut from lemon wax, tinge round the edge with light green. The leaves are rather narrow, not so dark as the crocus; made from double wax. The head of the pin is merely rolled down the centre: they are attached a short way down the stem.

THE PRIMROSE.

(Primula.) *Forsaken.*

"Look on these flowers! as o'er an altar, shedding
On Milton's page soft light from coloured urns—
They are the links man's heart to nature wedding,
When to her breast the prodigal returns.
"They are from lone, wild places—forests, dingles,
Fresh banks of many a low-voiced hidden stream;
Where the sweet star of eve looks down and mingles
Faint lustre with the water-lily's gleam."
Mrs. Hemans.

[18]

This unassuming pretty flower has a salver-shaped corolla; but in modelling it, I advise its being formed of five petals. Prepare the latter in double white wax, colour them upon both sides with my lemon powder (this is a most beautiful preparation), taking the precaution not to carry the same to the end, or it would prevent adhesion of the wax. With a small sable brush, form a triangular spot of deep yellow at the lower end of the broad part of the petal. Attach to the end of a second-size wire a piece of lemon wax, extending the same half an inch down the stem; this is to form a foundation: the point is to be neatly moulded, and to be seen peeping, as it were, from the centre of the flower. The petals are curled in the following manner;—rest the petal in the palm of the left hand, placing the side that has the triangular spot downwards, press the third finger of the right hand in the centre, and then upon the opposite side strongly indent with the point of the pin. Place the five petals thus prepared round the stem previously formed, press the petals neatly together, flattening them down a little to give the appearance of being formed in one piece. The calyx is cut in very light green wax, it is in one piece, vandyked at the top into five points; in each point press the pin, and attach it afterwards round the neck or tube of the flower. Wash the calyx with a weak solution of gum water, using for the purpose a sable brush. Sprinkle it over, while moist, with a little of my prepared down. The stem should look transparent, consequently the wire must be covered with very light green or lemon wax. For the leaf, see my general instructions upon foliage.

[19]

VIOLET.

(Viola Odorata.) *Modesty.*

"As the dew that moistens the rose at dawn,
Gives the Violet many a tear,
So bright in the morning of life she shone,
That her fragrance still lives while her spirit is gone,
Embalming her memory here."
M'Comb.
"Sweet flower! spring's earliest, loveliest gem;
While other flowers are idly sleeping,
Thou rear'st thy purple diadem,
Meekly from thy seclusion peeping.
"Thou, from the little secret mound,
Where diamond dew-drops shine above thee,
Scatterest thy modest fragrance round;
And well may nature's poet love thee!
"Thine is a short, swift reign, I know,
But love, thy spirit still pervading,
New violet tufts again shall blow,
Then fade away as thou art fading;
"And be renewed;—the hope how blest,
(Oh, may that hope desert me never!)
Like thee, to sleep on nature's breast,
And wake again, to bloom for ever!"
Bowring.
"A violet, by a mossy stone—
Half hidden from the eye;
Fair as a star, when only one
Is shining in the sky."
Wordsworth.

Prepare the petals in white wax: there are five in number. Pass the head of a large pin firmly down the centre, so as to cup each. Cover a fine green wire with a strip of light green wax; at the end of this affix a small piece of orange wax, and mould it to a point, not allowing it to be larger than a carraway seed. Dip the point of this foundation in water, and then [20] into the second yellow powder, which gives it the appearance of farina. Place three petals under the foundation, and the remaining two on the top, turning them back; bend the stalk up, and under the three petals place a small piece of white wax, which is to be coloured purple after it is attached. The calyx consists of five points, and are placed round the neck of the flower.

PURPLE VIOLETS.

"Violets, sweet tenants of the shade,
In purple's richest pride arrayed,
Your errand here fulfil;
Go, bid the artist's simple stain
Your lustre imitate in vain,
And match your Maker's skill."

Purple violets are constructed precisely the same as the former; the only difference that exists being that the petals require to be cut from blue wax, and painted upon both sides with purple (bright crimson and middle blue.)
"Like the sweet south
That breathes upon a bank of violets,
(So darkly, deeply, beautifully blue,)
Smelling and giving odours."
"Thou smiling promise of more sunny days,
How do I love thine unobtrusive glance!"

ANEMONE.

(Anemone Hortensis.) *Sickness.*

The petals are cut from thick or double white wax. Place a piece of fine white wire half way up each, and secure it to its position by placing a narrow strip of white wax upon the same, rolling it down each edge with the head of the smallest pin. [21] Colour them from the centre to the point with bright purple (second blue and bright crimson), the large brush to be used, (see my directions, p. 13 .) The small petals are cupped by laying each in the palm of the left hand, and pressing it firmly with the thumb of the right hand. The large or outside petals are curled in the same manner, but the points turned back. The centre or foundation is formed by passing two strips of double pink wax round the end of a strong wire, (care must be taken at all times to double the wire down to prevent its slipping;) mould the same to a point, leaving it broad at the lower end; indent it strongly round with the curling pin; colour this half way down with dark or black-looking purple, (dark blue and crimson.)

The stamina are also formed from pink wax: first roll a whip (as in muslin) which produces the anthers, and cut a fringe the third of an inch deep. Wind the same around the previously formed centre, and then brush them out with the dark purple brush that has been applied to the foundation. When thoroughly dry, touch the ends occasionally with green; this must be done with the sable brush. At the back of the pulp first formed, close to the wire, affix the small petals at equal distance, and the large ones, which turn back, in the intervening spaces. When the anemone is in bud, it is surrounded by a calyx, but as it expands it rises and leaves the said calyx at least one inch down the stem; it has a fringed appearance, and is prepared from double green wax. The stem is covered neatly with light green wax.

The anemones grow in great variety of colour, but this instruction, as to form and centre, is applicable to all. The brilliant scarlet and purple, contrasted with the pink, lemon, and white, form a pretty group by themselves.
[22]

TULIP VAN THOL.

(Tulipa Præcox.) *Declaration of Love.*

"Flowers are the brightest things which earth
On her broad bosom loves to cherish;
Gay they appear as children's mirth,
Like fading dreams of hope they perish."
Patterson.

Prepare the petals from double yellow wax, placing the shining sides together, a fine white wire half way up between. Form two distinct creases up the centre with the point of the pin; with the head of the latter cup the broad part of the petal. Turn the edges inward towards the point, and colour each petal upon both sides with the crimson powder, softening off the same, and leaving a margin of the yellow free from colour. The stamina are prepared (according to pattern), from double yellow wax, and painted with rich brown (cake sepia and crimson), from the broad part to the point. To a large wire affix a piece of double green wax, cover the same with lemon wax, and press it into a triangular form: place a strip of double green wax three quarters of an inch from this point, to form a foundation to attach the petals to. Place round the foundation the brown stamina previously prepared, and then attach the petals, in rows of three or five; they vary very much in number, some flowers being much more double than others.

The remarks in the foregoing instructions on the "Van Thol Tulip," are also applicable to the Summer Tulip; the centre is formed the same, but rather larger; nature must do the rest. The great beauty of the flower in the florist's eye, consists in its being cup-shaped and round at the base. The ground colour of the flower ought also to be very clear and bright in the centre.
[23]

NARCISSUS.

Permission.

"By all those token-flowers that tell
What words can ne'er express so well."
Byron.

Cut six petals in double white wax; indent up the centre of each with the point of a curling pin; press against this crease upon the opposite side, so as to produce a ribbed appearance. Pass the head of the curling pin down on each side of the previously named crease, and press the petals back. Cut a strip of yellow wax half an inch deep and one inch and a half in length; plait it up at one edge, and join it round to form a cup. To the end of a piece of middle size wire attach the stamina, draw the same through the cup, and fasten it underneath. Take a slip of pale green wax, and wind round the wire under the cup, to form the tube or neck of the flower. Attach three petals in a triangular form immediately under the cup, and the remaining three immediately between those preceding.

THE JONQUIL

is constructed precisely the same; but use for the petals double yellow wax instead of white, and orange wax for the cup instead of yellow.

THE DAISY.

(Bellis Perennis.) *Innocence.*

Whilst culling the sweet and early flowers, I cannot permit myself to pass the daisy, that pretty and simple production of nature, so emblematical of innocence, and which has been immortalized by poets, ancient and modern.
[24]
THE DAISY.
"A nymph demure, of lowly port,
Or sprightly maiden, of Love's court,
In thy simplicity the sport
Of all temptations;
A queen in crown of rubies dressed,
A starveling in a scanty vest,
Are all, as seems to suit thee best,
Thy appellations.
"I see thee glittering from afar,
And then thou art a pretty star;
Not quite so fair as many are
In heaven above thee;
Yet like a star, with glittering crest,
Self-poised, in air thou seem'st to rest—
May peace come never to his nest,
Who shall reprove thee.
"Sweet flower—for by that name at last,
When all my reveries are past,
I call thee, and to that cleave fast,
Sweet silent creature,
That breath'st with me in sun and air;
Do thou, as thou art wont, repair
My heart with gladness, and a share
Of thy meek nature."
Wordsworth.

The daisy may be made entirely white, crimson tipped, or crimson all over the petals: the latter are cut in single white wax, a strip at once the width of a sheet of wax. After the petals are coloured, the pin is deeply indented into each, some in fact are made quite round. The flower grows single and double, so that there is no decided number required; this must be left to the taste of the copyists; but if they prefer the double flower, the eye or centre is scarcely visible. On the contrary, if it is a single flower that is to be imitated, the eye must be increased. To form the latter, take a sheet of yellow wax, fold it at the end the eighth of an inch deep, hold it between the thumb and finger of the left hand, and with the [25] point of the curling pin indent the edge closely the whole length, and pass round the end of the middle wire, letting it rise a little in the centre. The petals are then attached very closely, and as many as form the double or single flower, whichever may be preferred. The calyx is green, and placed on similarly to the petals.
"Wee, modest, crimson-tipped flower
* * * * thou bonnie gem."
Burns.

WALL-FLOWER.

Fidelity in misfortune.

"How oft doth an emblem-bud silently tell
What language could never speak half so well."

Cut from bright orange four wax petals for each blossom: colour the edges, and vein each a rich brown (crimson powder and cake sepia). Press the finger in the centre of every petal, for the purpose of giving a crumpled appearance.

Use a piece of middle size wire; cover it with green wax, and affix to the end four stamina, made in the following manner: Double along the end of a sheet of lemon wax (a narrow fold); cut the stamina short and fine; colour the ends with my lemon powder. Place the petals immediately under; putting them on so as to form a square. The calyx is cut from green wax passed round the tube of the flower, and coloured afterwards with the same brush that has been used for the flower. The buds are made of solid wax; some green, others orange; and painted with the rich brown in various shades. In the largest buds, leave the orange points free from paint, at the point peeping from beneath the dark calyx.

There cannot be a more natural looking flower than the last described, if modelled neatly, and well in regard to colour; at the same time, I must remind my pupils that none can look worse if badly executed. [26]

Having now submitted what I consider a fair selection from spring flowers, I will proceed to those which we may observe at a later period, commencing with the rhododendron. This is one of a class of flowers which I admire most particularly in nature, and also find extremely useful in an artistic point of view. Its form is peculiarly eligible in grouping, and its value increased from the fact, that it is cultivated at the present time in such great varieties of shades and colours. I do not know that I can experience a greater treat than to visit the Botanical Gardens, Regent's Park, when their show of American plants is on view; and I would recommend my pupils to devote some time to perfect themselves in flowers that afford such great variety; and as instruction as to the formation of one conveys the same for all, except as to varying the colour, I do not feel that I could choose a more advantageous specimen of floriculture for imitation.

LILAC RHODODENDRON.

Danger.

"All are for use—for health—for pleasure given:—
All speak, in various ways, the bounteous hand of Heaven."
Charlotte Smith.

Cut the petals in white wax; chose it rather thick, but not the double wax. It is formed with two pieces, and yet when united it appears as if there were five petals. The colour is produced in any shade of lilac by mixing my bright crimson, middle blue, and a small portion of white together. This is laid on round the edge upon both sides with a large brush. When perfectly dry, the colour is partly taken off by passing a moist brush containing very little colour over the whole. This carries off the rough portion of the paint previously applied, and gives the petals a soft and shaded [27] appearance. Press the curling pin up the centre of each point, and pinch against it so as to form a distinct seam. Roll the head of the pin down each side of the seam, which will occasion the edges of the petal to look a little crumpled. Unite the petals neatly together, making a small plait between each. Form the pistil of double wax: thicken it at the end to represent the stigma. The stamina are produced by folding the end of a sheet of wax so as to produce the same appearance as a hem in muslin, and cut ten fine filaments for each flower (the hem represents the anthers). Colour the pistil and stamina pale pink: darken the end of the pistil to a deep crimson. Touch the ends of the stamina with a sable brush moistened with brown (crimson powder, orange powder, and cake sepia); while wet, dip them into farina (produced by mixing my lemon powder with white, quite dry). Cut a piece of wire, three inches long, middle size: pass a small piece of light green wax round the end, and double the wire down; then attach the pistil to it, and place the stamina round, taking care that the pistil rises above the stamina. The centre petal of each flower is dotted with brown, the same colour previously used for the anthers. The stem is passed through the centre of the corolla, pressing the edges of the latter neatly to the wire. It is one of those flowers that has not a calyx attached close to the flower, but is shaded lightly round the end with a crimson brush. The flowers are mounted in clusters, varying in number: seven form a pretty size. When the flowers are united, a cluster of small points of very light green wax are placed: these are what are termed by botanists, "calyx involucre," signifying that such calyx is remote from the flower. Place three or four leaves round the stem, a short distance from where the flowers are united.

Another of the American plants useful in grouping, is the

[28]

KALMIA.

(Latifolia.) *Combination.*

"Ye flowers of beauty, pencilled by the hand of God!"
Pollok.

The corolla is in one piece, having five points. It requires to be cut in thick wax. Press the finger in the centre, and pinch up each point, bending the same towards the centre. A double piece of wax, cut in points, is placed at the back; press the two firmly together, and make a hole in the centre with the large pin. Paint in the corolla a small circle of crimson points, using for this purpose a sable brush. Cover a piece of fine wire two inches in length; mould to the end a small piece of double green wax, making it quite round. The pistil is affixed to this, and is formed by rolling the edge of the wax (as a whip in muslin), and cutting it fine, as previously directed. The stamina are prepared in the same manner, consisting of ten filaments, and are placed round the pistil. Pass the stalk through the centre of the corolla, rendering it secure by pressing the fingers close to the flower underneath. Finish off the flower by attaching five minute points of green wax. After the pistil and stamina are drawn through the flower, press the anther of each filament down to the corolla with the head of the pin, and tip them with deep crimson.

YELLOW JASMINE.

(Jasminum Revolutum.) *Grace and Elegance.*

Cut the petals from double yellow wax. There are five to each flower. Pass the head of the small curling pin quickly twice down each petal; and indent it strongly down the narrow or tube part of each petal upon the opposite side. Cover a piece of fine wire, about three inches long; affix a small piece of green wax, pressed into a point by the side of, and at [29] the end of, the said points. Dip the latter into water, and while wet, into the yellow powder, to represent farina. Place the five petals around, pressing each on neatly and firmly, permitting the points or stamina to be seen just rising from the neck or tube of the flower. Pass a small piece of green wax round the lower end of the tube to form the calyx. Some buds may be formed from wax, wound round wire, and made solid; others of petals closed. About four flowers, and three or four buds, form a pretty and useful cluster; but the number may be increased or diminished at pleasure.

WHITE JASMINE.

(Jasminum Officinale.) *Amiableness.*

The petals are prepared from thick or double white wax. It is put together precisely as the last named flower; but the petals are pointed, instead of being round, as in the yellow. Press the point of the curling pin up the centre of each petal. After the flower is united, the tube is tinged, first with pale yellow, and subsequently with red, very slightly. The calyx consists of five fine points, which are cut in green wax, and attached at the bottom of the tube. The flowers are mounted like the yellow jasmine. The green sprigs are placed on two at once, facing each other.

CAPE JASMINE.

(Gardenia.) *Sweetness.*

The petals are cut in thick wax, or single wax doubled; when the latter is the case, be careful to place the two shining sides together. It is particularly easy to form: the petals require to be curled precisely as the yellow jasmine. The centre is formed by crushing two or three small pieces of orange wax to the point of a wire. The first five small petals are very faintly tinged with orange; this is merely to [30] give warmth to the centre of the flower, to make up for the deficiency of the life-glow, if I may use this term—great care must therefore be taken not to make it too dark. All the succeeding petals are placed on in rows of five, turning some of the petals forward towards the centre of the flower.

The neck of the flower is already formed from the ends of the petals; it only requires to be moulded very smooth, and coloured a light pomona green. The calyx consists of five points of green wax, placed at the end of the tube. The dark foliage is placed round in clusters, and produces a pleasing contrast to the flower. I would here observe, that this flower is particularly useful in grouping. It is a greenhouse production, and extremely fragrant in nature; it is consequently always consistent to place it in a bouquet; independently of this, it is an excellent substitute for white camellia in groups, where the last named flower would be too large.

I shall proceed to give some instruction in Roses. The varieties now grown and named in our nurseries amount to the almost incredible number of two thousand. I shall therefore choose, for the information and improvement of those ladies who kindly think proper to place themselves under the guidance of my little book, about six kinds, such as I deem most useful, and as being different in form and colour. I think, when these are perfectly understood, any other kind can be copied easily from nature. I shall commence with the old favourite,

THE CABBAGE OR PROVENCE ROSE.

(Rosa Centifolia.) *Beauty.*

"The rose has one powerful virtue to boast
Above all the flowers of the field—
When its leaves are all dead, and fine colours are lost,
Still how sweet a perfume it will yield."
Watts.

[31] Cut the petals from pale pink wax; colour the three smallest rather deep with the crimson powder. The split petals, marked on my pattern fifteen, are coloured the same, but rather a lighter hue. Each succeeding set are painted the same, but gradually diminish the colour until you arrive at the outer petals, which are the lightest of all. To form the petals, use a pin as little as possible; cupping them with the thumb or finger, according to its size. For the largest petals, use the thumb, so pressing each in the centre, while it is resting in the palm of the left hand, as to become perfectly round. The last two or outer rows are turned back with the head of a curling pin.

Prepare the foundation of solid wax, rolled round the end of a moderate size wire. It must be cone-shaped. The three smallest petals are crushed and placed at the point in a triangular form. The split petals, marked on my pattern fifteen, are united into clusters of five, and placed round immediately under the three that are crushed. Each succeeding row of petals are placed on in like manner, taking care that each petal is attached to the under part of the foundation, and not upon the side. I particularly name this, as I too frequently find ladies err in forming the roundness of the rose. The last two rows of petals, which are turned back, must be placed rather lower than those preceding. The calyx is cut from double light green wax.

The head of the curling pin is passed down the centre of each point previously to their being placed on. Pass a strip of double green wax close round the base of the flower, moulding it round and smooth with the thumb and finger. This is to represent the seed cup. When the calyx is affixed, it must rest against the back of the rose, and be so neatly moulded over the seed cup, as not to show any division or seam. [32]

THE MOSS ROSE.

Beauty and Love.

Is similarly constructed (being one of the same class), but is rather smaller. It requires the addition of a little real moss. It must be the fine spray moss; and dried quickly, by placing a warm flat-iron upon it. It is affixed to the calyx and seed cup by pressing it on with the head of the curling pin.

THE WHITE ROSE.

(Rose Alba.) *Silence.*

Cut the petals from thin white wax. Tinge the lower part of the first three sets of petals with my lemon powder. Cup all the petals with the finger, turning the last or largest two rows back. Cut a few stamina in lemon wax, with the edge rolled to form the anthers; colour them with orange, and when quite dry, touch them occasionally with brown (crimson powder and cake sepia). These stamina are divided into clusters, eight or ten filaments in each, and about five in number. Make a small cone-shaped foundation; attach one cluster of stamina at the point. The ten small petals are affixed round, turning in various directions, and interspersed with the rest of the stamina. The whole of the remaining petals are placed on five in a row, the last two turning back. Finish off with calyx and seed cup, as in previous instruction. This rose is peculiarly adapted for bridal bouquets; and I must here mention, while alluding to the subject of bridal favours, that I made upwards of ten thousand of these roses upon the happy occasion of Her Majesty's marriage. It may afford some trivial amusement to my younger friends, to relate the following anecdote, in connection with the event just alluded to. About three years after Her Majesty was united to His Royal [33] Highness Prince Albert, a gentleman visited my establishment, and inspected my specimens of flowers in wax with evident satisfaction. He represented himself as being a great admirer of wax-work generally; and stated, that he himself possessed a rare specimen, in fact, a perfect *bijou*. He should wish me to see it. I, of course, expressed some anxiety to behold such perfection of art; and accordingly, he sent his footman with a small box, charged with strict orders to be particularly careful in conveying the same. After removing sundry pieces of tissue paper, and as many of wadding, my surprise may be easily imagined, when I beheld one of the identical bouquets (white rose, orange blossom, and myrtle, tied with white satin ribbon) that I had myself manufactured upon the joyous occasion already alluded to. I am but human nature, therefore, I hope I may be pardoned for expressing and feeling a certain degree of vanity upon inspecting this Royal relic of my own hands; still, I am not blind to the fact, that the happy occasion for which the bouquet had been prepared, namely, the nuptials of our beloved Sovereign, had materially enhanced its value to the possessor;—but I will no longer digress from the leading feature of this work, but commence the description of the formation of

THE DAMASK ROSE.

(Rosa Damascena.) *Freshness of Complexion.*

"The rose, like ruddy youth, in beauty stands,
And would be cropped by none but fairest hands."
Cut the petals from white wax, and paint them upon both sides (with my crimson), two-thirds down. Cup the petals as in the preceding rose. Cut two strips of stamina in lemon wax, tip them with my orange powder. Make a foundation of lemon wax, and pass round the strips already mentioned. Place in a triangular form the six small petals in clusters of [34] two; the next two sets are attached in like manner at the intermediate spaces, the rest of the petals are placed on singly, five in each row, the largest to turn back: finish off with seed cup and calyx as before named. It is particularly necessary that the smallest or internal petals should not be coloured too low down, as the white in the centre gives great relief to the flower.

SWEET-SCENTED TEA ROSE.

(Rosa Safrano.) *Charming.*

The petals of this rose require to be cut in thick white wax, coloured three parts down with my lemon powder; shade lightly over this, but not quite to the edge, with a little of my second yellow, and finish off by a light tint of crimson (crimson lake in cake.) The petals are deep and few, and require a great deal of cupping; to assist in producing this rotundity of petal use the head of the ivory pin, commencing to roll from the bottom to about half-way up the petal. Make a foundation of white wax, rather large and cone-shaped; colour it the same as petals; place the latter on singly, and press them forward to meet at the point and conceal the foundation. They are placed on five in a row, and the last two turned back: the seed cup is rather small; the calyx, and the back petals are all deeply coloured with crimson. The stem is also very red.

YELLOW ROSE.

(Rosa. Cloth of Gold.) *Infidelity.*

"The rose is fragrant, but it fades in time."—Dryden.
Cut the petals from light lemon wax, colour them with deep yellow towards the lower end, gradually shading off the same towards the upper end of each petal. The first three [35] sets of petals are placed on in clusters of five, the others singly in rows of five. The foundation is made similar to the damask rose, and the stamina show from the front of the flower. Calyx and seed cup formed as usual.
J. Gardner & C. Lith. 86 Hatton Garden.

AUSTRIAN BRIAR ROSE.

(Rosa Lutea.) *Mingled Pleasure and Pain.*

This is a showy single flower, and very easily and quickly accomplished. There are but five petals, cut from bright yellow wax; colour them half-way down each with crimson: cup them a little in the palm of the hand, not using a pin at all. The foundation is rather small, and

formed of green wax—one strip of stamina placed round, cut in lemon wax, tipped with orange powder. Calyx and seed cup formed according to previous instruction.

Having given as many roses as my space will admit of, and as will be required for the purpose of initiating learners in this kind of flower, I will turn the attention of my readers to another class, held in much esteem, and which will afford a wide field of variety to copyists. I allude to

THE CARNATION.

(Dianthus.) *Pure Love.*

"Yon bright carnation—once thy cheek
Bent o'er it in the bud;
And back it gives thy blushes meek
In one rejoicing flood!"

This may be made in three varieties. The flakes are striped with broad bands of colour, the bizarres are striped with three colours, and the picotees have a narrow margin of [36] streaks and spots; they are all painted with a sable brush. To enable the wax to take the fine pencil marks, moisture from the lips must be conveyed with the finger to the petal. Make the strokes or bands broad near the edge of the petal, and gradually diminish them to a fine point towards the lower end. The petals are curled as follows:—press each in the palm of the left hand, and roll the head of the pin twice or three times down the painted side of the petal, taking care to do so between, and not upon the stripes. Roll the pin once up the back of the petal, commencing from the bottom, and not extending the same above half-way up. Cover the stem with green wax, and place the petals on in rows of five. The calyx is cut from double wax (light green); it is in one piece, with five points. It is shaded rather dark green in the centre, and the points tipped with red (very faint.) It is passed round the tube of the flower; at the base of the same affix six small pieces of wax, as scales.

The leaf is long and narrow, cut from double wax, and a fine wire covered and placed between to support it. To give it the natural bloom, pass it through the prepared arrowroot. The leaves are placed on the stem two and two, to face each other, and a small piece of lemon wax passed round, to represent the joint that is always visible in this flower.

MYRTLE.

(Myrtus Communis.) *Love.*

This flower is always admired in a bouquet from its light and pretty appearance, and is in nature very fragrant. Cut the petals, five in number, of double wax, indent the head of a curling pin in each; cut a fringe at the end of a thin sheet of white wax, having previously folded a very small piece down to form the anthers. Wind this strip or fringe round the end [37] of the finest wire, taking care to double the latter down. Brush these filaments all out, and tip them at the points with my lemon powder: place the five petals round. The calyx is a row of small points cut in light green wax; the points are touched with a brush containing a little brown, and then passed once round the flower. The stalk is covered with a light green, but partially coloured with brown also. The buds are made very round, of solid wax, and a calyx affixed to them like the flower. To make the foliage, look at my instructions. Commence mounting the flower at the top of a wire; four or six leaves must be attached first, two and two, then the buds in like order, leaves under each, and lastly the flowers. About four or six make a pretty spray.

HONEYSUCKLE.

(Caprifolium.) *Devoted Affection.*

Colour eight or ten blossoms with second yellow, two or three are left white, being all cut from wax devoid of colour; shade them with crimson lake in cake; cut a piece of fine wire, two inches long, cut a strip of white wax, three quarters of an inch in length, and pass it round one end of the wire. This is to form the tube or foundation for the stamina to be attached to: the latter are cut very fine from double lemon wax. The anthers are tipped orange, the pistil green. Affix the pistil and five stamina to each foundation, and then enclose it in the tube or long part of the petals previously coloured, as also in the white blossoms, first having passed a small head pin twice or thrice down each. The tube is coloured dark crimson, gradually softened off towards the upper end of the blossom. A calyx is attached at the base of the tube in the form of a small cup—a piece of double green wax, cut very narrow, and passed once round. The buds are made solid: [38] cut the wax, which must be double, in a triangular form; by so doing, and winding the broadest end round the corresponding end of the wire, the proper form will be easily accomplished, without much assistance from the fingers. Unite all the buds together first, and then place the blossoms round. The leaves are placed on two and two.

THE FUCHSIA;

(Fulgens;) *Good taste:*

Will afford a pleasing variety to the flowers already described. Its blossoms hang pendant like a tassel; it is both graceful in form, and brilliant in colour: its construction is simple, being formed from two patterns only. The smallest is cut in single lemon wax, the largest in double wax, the same colour. The four points of the largest pattern are tipped with green, and shaded off with light scarlet towards the upper part of the tube. It is not, however, entirely coloured until it is made, as it is always difficult to unite a tube flower if it is painted too close to the edge. The head of the curling pin is rolled up each point upon the inside, and the tube formed with the handle of a brush, joining the wax neatly upon one side. After it is united, it is again painted with my scarlet powder and a small portion of the crimson.

The small or inner petals are coloured upon both sides with bright crimson only. The head of a large curling pin is passed once down. The stamina are cut from double lemon wax, a whip, as in muslin, being first rolled to produce the anthers; these are touched with gum water, and, while wet, dipped into cream colour powder, (produced by the combination of my lemon and white.) The pistil is the same as the stamina, only that it extends to a greater length: the stamina and pistil are shaded very light scarlet. Cover a piece of fine [39] wire, about four inches in length, with light green wax, mould to the end a strip of lemon wax, to which affix first the pistil and subsequently the stamina. Pass the wire through the tube, and fix it firmly at the end; a narrow strip of double light green wax placed once round the base of the tube completes the whole. The buds are made solid, and formed similarly to the honeysuckle; they are shaded green and scarlet, like the flower.

THE RED FUCHSIA;

(Fuchsia,) *Taste:*

Is cut from white wax. It consists of four purple petals, and four crimson; these are painted with the large brush upon both sides, leaving a short space free from colour towards the base of each. Cut the pistil and eight stamina as previously directed, and colour them with crimson. To the end of these may be observed in nature small particles of farina, this is produced (as in the former instruction of fuchsia fulgens), by dipping them while moistened with gum water into dry powder. A foundation is formed at the end of a piece of fine wire, the pistil attached, and the stamina encircling the same. The four purple petals are then placed on to form a square, having the head of the curling pin previously rolled down each to cup them a little. The crimson or outer petals are curled in like manner, and placed precisely at the corners where the inner petals unite. The flower is now complete, with the exception of the seed cup; but previous to this being placed on, (which is merely a piece of green wax moulded into the shape of a small berry,) the flower is coloured again crimson, softening it off towards the said seed cup.

[40]

FORGET ME NOT.

Forget me not.

"The very name is Love's own poetry,
Born of the heart, and of the eye begot,
Nursed amid sighs and smiles of constancy,
And ever breathing—'Love! forget me not.'"
Miller.

This little flower is cut in one piece from thick white wax. A hole is pierced in the centre with the curling pin. The finest white wire is used: affix a small piece of wax to the end, and fold it down with the wire; it must be very minute. Pass it through the front of the flower, and fasten it at the back by moulding it gently with the point of the pin. It is painted after it is made: the centre is touched with a sable brush— the colour, second yellow. The edges of the flower are coloured a brilliant blue, for which use the light blue, with minute portions of white and crimson. The buds and opening flowers are more pink than the full-blown flowers.

PINK GERANIUM.

(Pelargonium.) *Preference.*

Cut the petals in thick white wax; there are three narrow and two broad. Mix a little white powder with some crimson, and paint all the petals half way down lightly with this colour. The brush must contain but a very small portion of colour, or it would dry rough. The broad petals are afterwards coloured as follows:—first vein the lower ends with cake smalt and crimson, using for the purpose a fine sable brush. Then take [41] a large brush, containing crimson alone, and form a large round spot, gradually shading it off towards each edge. When thoroughly dry, apply in the same manner the colour first used for veining, leaving a light margin of the rose colour previously laid on. With a sable brush paint some very faint pink veins, extending from the spot towards (but not quite touching) the ends of the petals. Some dark veins are laid on the spot also with crimson powder and cake sepia. The middle size wire is necessary to support the flower. Commence its construction by affixing a strip of white wax about an inch down the same; this is to represent the pistillum. Five very fine points extend beyond the end of the wire, these are previously snipped with the scissors; they are termed in botany the stigma. At the base of the pistillum pass a strip of green wax; this is the foundation to which the stamina and petals are to be attached. The pistillum and stigma are painted entirely over with the same colour previously used for veining. Cut five fine stamina in white wax, to the points of each attach an anther, cut in deep orange wax. They are placed across the end, and united by pressing them together with the head of the curling pin. Curl the broad petals by laying the painted side next the hand and pressing the thumb into its centre. Upon the opposite side at the lower end of the petal indent and round it with the point of the pin. The small petals are similarly curled, although it is necessary to vary them a little according to taste; for upon observing nature it will be found that there is no formality, in fact scarcely two petals or two flowers are precisely the same upon a tree or stem. Attach the stamina to the foundation, and then the two broad petals; finally, the three narrowest are placed immediately under the stamina. The calyx is cut from light green wax. The head of the pin is to curl each previous to its being placed behind the petals. It is shaded rather dark green towards the stem. Wash the calyx over with a weak solution of gum water, and sprinkle it [42] with down. In laying on the latter do not touch it with the fingers, but throw it on from the bottle, and shake off all that does not adhere.

SCARLET GERANIUM.

Comforting.

The petals are cut from thick white wax. Colour them upon both sides with bright scarlet (scarlet and crimson both in powders), form a very small foundation of white wax to the end of a fine wire. Cut five fine and short stamina, place them on the foundation, and colour them red. Affix the five petals round, the two largest placed uppermost, the three smaller ones under. Attach calyx as in the former flower. Cover the stem neatly with light green wax, and mount the flowers in clusters. Make some buds moulded in light green wax, others in white wax, painted scarlet at the points; and the calyx placed round as in the flower.

MIGNONETTE.

(Reseda Odorata.) *Unconscious Beauty.*

It is a singular circumstance that in this country this fragrant production of nature is known by a French name, the translation of which is the "little darling," while in Paris it is only known by its Latin appellation, *reseda*, (herb, or dock cresses); but I believe I am correct in stating that its seeds were first conveyed into England from Paris. It is not particularly difficult to form, but requires extremely good sight, and a light touch in its construction. It is of course made without a paper pattern, and I would recommend a natural flower always to be taken as a copy. It is also necessary to be very particular as to the lemon tint used, the orange, and the shade of green, for [43] if the flower is formed correctly, it still looks unnatural if these points are not materially considered.

Take a sheet of lemon wax, very thin and not too new; cut directly from the corner six or eight fine filaments, as pointed as possible; roll them into a small cluster. It requires two clusters of this size, and two others nearly the same, but shorter. Fold the end of a piece of lemon wax, and snip (very short) a few stamina, which appear, when coloured, like seed. The colour required is a sort of pinky orange, if I may be allowed to use such a term; for which purpose I employ my second orange, white, and a minute portion of crimson powder: of course it requires some judgment as to the several quantities. Commence the formation by attaching a small piece of green wax to the end of a stem made from white wire, mould it round according to nature; under this place the cluster of orange seeds, on the top a small portion of lemon wax, and at each corner the largest cluster of lemon stamina; the smaller clusters place at the corners and under the orange seeds. The calyx consists of five very narrow strips of green wax, placed neatly and regularly at the back of the flower. Cover the stem with very light green wax.

ORANGE BLOSSOM.

(Citrus.) *Chastity.*

This is cut in double white wax. It consists of five petals. The head of the small curling pin is passed up and down over the whole of each; the petals are afterwards curled a little with the fingers, to do away with any formality. A middle size wire is used; pass a strip of white wax round, about half an inch in length; press it broad at the end, and then place a fringe of stamina twice round: colour the end of the pistil and stamina with light orange. The petals are next affixed, [44] and a cup or calyx is formed at the base of light green wax. The buds are moulded solid, round at the end, and pinched up into rather an irregular form towards the base. The calyx is finished off the same as the flower.

SERINGA.

Counterfeit.

"The sweet seringa, yielding but in scent
To the rich orange."

Cut the petals in white wax, double or thick; there are but four to form the corolla. They are curled precisely like the orange blossom. The centre is also similar to the last named, only that there is no pistil or enlargement amongst the stamina. The calyx consists of four points of double green wax, indented with the pin, and tipped brown. Each point is placed at the back of each petal.

LILY.

(Lilium Candidum.) *Purity of heart.*

"Observe the rising lily's snowy grace."—Thomson.

The lily is an advantageous flower in a large group. The one I am going first to notice is peculiar for its purity of colour; it is very ornamental in a garden, and is much revered in Catholic countries. Painters frequently place it in the hands of the Virgin.

The petals, six in number, are cut from double white wax: the broad or inner petals are curled as follows:—pass the head of the smallest curling pin all over the petal to make it [45] look slightly ribbed. Press the pin firmly up the centre to make a distinct crease; turn the petal, and press against the crease upon each side so as to form a groove. Return to the former side, and again press the pin against the two outside edges of the previously made creases; you will now have produced two ribs or ridges. Pass the head of the pin round the edge of the petal, to render it thin in appearance and to stretch the same. This will also enable you to curl the petal into form with the fingers, without splitting the edges. The outer or narrow petals are curled similarly; but the slight difference there exists between the two will be better understood by taking a real flower to model from. Cover a piece of middle size wire with light green wax, to represent the pistillum: enlarge it with the same at the upper end to represent the stigma; press it into a triangular form, and indent it with the point of the pin. Six stamina are placed round; they are each formed in the following manner:—cover a piece of fine white wire with white wax, this is a filament; attach to the end an anther, formed of bright orange wax, indent it strongly across with the point of the pin. Wash it over with gum water, and while it is in a state of moisture plunge it into the orange coloured powder. The three largest petals are placed on first, the three smaller or outer petals at the intervening spaces.

THE LILIUM LANCIFOLIUM.

Generous heart.

The petals of this flower are curled similarly to the former, but they bend back more in the form of a Turk's cap. There is a narrow strip of bright yellow-green wax placed in the centre, and at the lower end of each petal. The petals are painted light pink (crimson and white), and covered with rich [46] crimson spots. The roughness at the lower end of each petal is produced by cutting small pieces of double white wax, and pressing them on with the head of the pin. The pistillum and stamina are also formed in the same manner as the *lilium candidum*, but vary in colour. The filaments of the stamina are green, the anthers rich brown, produced with crimson and cake sepia.

WHITE WATER-LILY.

(Nymphea Alba.) *Eloquence.*

"Where will they stop, those breathing powers,
The spirits of the new-born flowers?
They wander with the breeze, they wind
Where'er the streams a passage find."
Wordsworth.

Commence the foundation of this flower by passing five strips of double yellow wax round the end of a strong wire, indenting the edge of each with the point of the curling pin, and pressing the same into a flat surface: this foundation must be about three quarters of an inch in diameter. Cut sixteen strips of very deep orange wax (double), about the tenth of an inch in width: place them round at equal distances. Cut the pattern No. 1, in double yellow wax. Roll the head of the curling pin in the broad part, and bend the point of the same back. Place these on in rows of eight, taking care that each row is between those preceding. The petals are cut in thick white wax: cup them with the large head ivory pin, to give them a rotundity of form; these are all placed on in rows of four. Under the two or three largest sets it is essential to place a small piece of white wire (covered with wax), to support each petal. The four outside petals [47] are green externally and white within; this is accomplished by pressing a sheet of thin green wax against the thick white. They are shaded brown up the centre upon the green side, using for the purpose the large brush, slightly moistened with carmine and sepia. The stem requires to be thickly covered with light green wax, shaded with brown, similar to the back of the flower.

THE YELLOW WATER-LILY.

Retirement.

Is much more simple to form. It consists of only five petals; these are cut in double yellow wax; colour them rather lightly with green upon both sides, from the centre towards the base of each. Curl the petals with the head of the large pin until they become deeply cupped. The centre is much smaller than that of the white lily—not exceeding in diameter the third of an inch. The stamina are produced by cutting three or four narrow strips of double yellow wax, and passing them round the foundation; they must not extend above it, but when brushed out form a full daisy-like centre. The five petals are attached to the back of these, and the stem finished off as the last.

THE BLUE WATER-LILY;

Warm affection;

Forms a pleasing variety, but is not so generally well known, from the fact of its requiring care in cultivation. Those previously described may be seen blowing luxuriantly in common ponds; but this I am about to give instruction upon I have never seen except in a hot-house. [48]

Cut the petals in thick white wax; attach a fine white wire half-way up the back of each. Colour them upon both sides with light blue, or more properly speaking with blue lavender. It is a peculiar shade of colour produced by mixing the light blue powder with white and a minute portion of crimson. Curl the petals with the head of a large curling pin, by passing it firmly once down each centre. The four outside petals are green at the back, and shaded rather darker up the centre with the same colour. The centre is formed similar to the white lily, but not so large. The stamina are cut also in double yellow wax, and arranged regularly round in rows of sixteen; three rows of these are sufficient. The petals are placed on four in a row throughout the flower; the stem is moderately thick and green.

DAHLIA.

(Dahlia Purpurea.) *Instability.*

Cut the required number of petals from pink wax—colour them upon both sides with crimson. When quite dry, wash them over lightly with bright purple (using for the purpose a large brush, very moist.) When a second colour requires to be laid on, I use a small portion of cake colour, (in the present instance cake crimson, lake, with middle blue in powder.) To curl the petals press the pin once down the centre, upon the shining side; turn the petal, and press against the same at the point, forming a melon-shaped section. Fold the edges of the petal to meet at the lower end.

Make a foundation of two strips of double wax, taking care to double in the wire. Indent it strongly with the pin towards the point, as it must be pressed into a conical form: it must be one inch deep and as much in circumference. Cut three strips of double wax, vandyke them with the scissors, [49] and indent each point with the pin, bend the whole forward, and paint them in the same manner and colour as the petals. Pass these strips round the foundation first, keeping them exactly the same height. Place three rows of petals on, seven in number, then increase them to nine in a row, and so continue until the flower is complete. Take care to place every petal between and not behind its predecessors, and let each row fall back, so that at the conclusion it has a globular appearance in front, and flat at the back of the flower. Cut the calyx in double wax; it consists of ten points, five are light green, attached to the back of the flower, and five dark sepals which are pendant round the stem.

THE SALVIA PATENS.

Rich and Rare.

This flower is of so rich and lovely a

hue, that for its colour alone it deserves imitation. There are but few decidedly blue flowers, and I do not myself know any one that approaches this for brilliancy; it is however useful in consequence of its form being light and spray-like. The petals require to be cut in double blue wax; the shape must be produced previously to the colour being laid on. Petals cut from pattern No. 1, are much rolled with the pin and neatly united up the back. Take a piece of middle size wire, with a small piece of wax secured at the end, and pass it through the opening of the tube just formed. The under or banner petal is formed by pressing it in the palm of the hand; turn up the edges of the broad end of the petal, and turn down the edges of the narrow part; at the same time I must mention that a small wire is placed between this petal, by which it is affixed to its position. The buds are formed in the same manner as the flower, with the exception of the banner petal. The calyx [50] consists of two points or sepals, attached one under and the other opposite the tube. The whole is painted with deep rich blue, produced by mixing cake smalt with the middle blue in powder. They are mounted in a spray by placing buds and flowers down the stem, two facing each other, and arranged alternate ways. A green leaf is placed under each bud and blossom.

VARIEGATED CAMELLIA.

Unpretending excellence.

"In eastern lands they talk of flowers,
And they tell in a garland their loves and cares;
Each blossom that blooms in their garden bowers,
On its leaves a mystic language bears."
J. G. Percival.

As the limits of this little work will not admit of my giving instruction in more than one of these favourite flowers, I select the variegated one, considering it the most difficult.

The petals require to be cut in thick wax; colour them upon both sides with bright crimson, leaving white circular spots indiscriminately in various parts of two petals out of every five. The largest petals are formed by pressing the thumb very firmly upon the shining side, taking care that the edge inclines back without any wrinkled appearance. A crease is made up the centre upon the opposite side. Each set of petals are painted and curled the same, but the smallest are folded together. The stamina must be prepared from pale lemon wax, (cut double,) and the anthers at the end tipped with orange powder to represent the farina; they are cut into small clusters of seven or eight. Use the large wire,—pass a piece of double wax, the width of a sheet, and half an inch in depth, round the wire,—about half an inch deep; bend the [51] wire down, and mould the whole into a cone shape. Affix a small cluster of stamina to the point, and in various directions the five smallest petals; insert among these two or three clusters of the stamina. Place in rows of five each succeeding set of petals, taking care in each row to introduce about two of the variegated or spotted petals, allowing such to be principally upon one side of the flower (and this may be observed in nearly all flowers that are variegated.)

The calyx is cut from lemon wax, shaded green and also brown. The head of the pin is rolled upon each to cup it: they are placed immediately behind the flower in rows of three, each succeeding set in the intervening spaces.

The stem is covered with a strip of light green wax, moulded smooth with the thumb and finger, tinged brown with the brush.

THE PASSION FLOWER;

Belief:

"Has become strangely interwoven with our faith, from a fancied resemblance to a cross and a crown, although it requires a great effort of the imagination to call up either the one or the other. Still its very name in some measure renders it sacred to faith and belief."

Cut the petals, ten in number, from treble wax, one of white and two of lemon; colour the lemon side with light green, leaving the edge rather lighter. Curl each petal in the following manner: press it in the hand, while warm, that the three thicknesses of wax may be certain to adhere. Roll the head of the small pin once down the centre upon the white side, and round the edge also. This must be done lightly at first, for if a pin is pressed too heavily it occasions the sheets of wax to separate and have a blistered appearance. Cut [52] three triangular pieces of double wax, one inch in length, place the broad end to a piece of fine wire, and mould them smoothly down, small at the base and broad at the point; these three are affixed to the end of a middle size wire, and painted purple after they are attached. A piece of light green wax is moulded round immediately under them; about a quarter of an inch from this is attached the stamina, cut in light green wax, and touched round the ladle shape end with my orange powder. A full inch from this is placed a small foundation, formed of strips of green wax, two of which are snipped and coloured purple. The rays are attached immediately afterwards, and are manufactured as follows:—cut a number of strips of white wax, roll them between the fingers to incline them to be round; place your pieces of marble in warm water, and finish rolling the said strips of wax or rays between them: this is a much quicker, easier, and cleaner process than by doing them entirely with the fingers. Cut a strip of double green wax to pattern, place it about three quarters of an inch from the edge of a folded paper, place each of the rays closely upon this, taking care that every point extends only to the paper; this method will enable you to place them perfectly even, which is very necessary. For a flower it requires two strips of these rays; they are painted blue at the point and purple at the base, leaving a corresponding space white between the two colours. Press the two strips neatly round the previously made foundation, bending them back and regulating them with the point of the curling-pin. I next attach five petals at equal distance, the longest and narrowest of the two sets are placed on first, the other five immediately between. The calyx is cut in light green wax, it consists of three sepals, which are rolled with the head of the pin and attached to the back of the flower. [53]

LEMON HOLLYHOCK.

Persuasion.

This flower should be constructed of very thin lemon wax. It requires thirty small petals and seven large for a full blown flower: each petal is shaded with the light yellow powder towards the lower end. Crimp each petal with the point of the curling pin, and fold one end forward, the other back. Pass a strip of double lemon wax round the end of a piece of middle size wire, and mould the same to a point; the thirty small petals are attached first, so as to form a full rosette. The large petals are affixed to the back, and finished off with the calyx of double green. Half blown flowers are formed the same, but cut from smaller patterns. The early buds are moulded solid of green wax, covered with lemon; the calyx is placed on similar to the flower, moistened with gum water and sprinkled with down. Pink hollyhocks may be made precisely the same, the only difference being that pink wax and colour must be substituted for lemon.

THE CACTUS.

Warmth.

Cut the petals in bright orange wax, place a fine white wire half way up each, and occasion it to adhere by attaching a strip of orange wax over it. Colour them upon both sides with carmine. Curl the petals by passing the head of the pin twice or thrice from each edge towards the centre, and bend the same back. Fold down the edge or end of two sheets of thick white wax. Leave a quarter of an inch from the end quite white, then paint a pink stripe half an inch deep; leave [54] again a quarter of an inch white, and finally finish with a stripe of green. Cut the whole two widths into a deep fringe to form the stamina, and colour the anthers (produced by the fold) with cream colour (white and lemon powders). Take a piece of middle size wire, pass round it a strip of white wax; this is to form the pistillum. Attach to the end five fine points of white wax, and paint them also cream colour; shade the filament of the pistillum red. Divide the stamina, attach half to the upper, and the remainder to the three under petals. Join the pistillum to a strong stem, passing white wax round to form a foundation. Affix to the foundation the six petals, to which are attached the stamina, letting the latter fall from the top petals over the lower ones, and dividing it so as to enable the pistillum to pass through. Every set of petals are placed precisely between those preceding until the flower is complete. It must be remembered that the largest petals are attached first, and that they gradually decrease until you arrive at the smallest.

"For not, oh, not alone to charm our sight,
Gave God your blooming forms, your leaves of light."
Charles Swain.

GROUPING FLOWERS.

One of the principle rules to be observed is to avoid placing those flowers together which approach the same form or colour. Thus, in arranging two round flowers, I invariably break the formality by introducing some light spray. To facilitate a taste for grouping is the cause of my introducing illustrations to this work. It will be observed that I arrange spring flowers always alone. I am not so particular with the flowers of every season, for art in cultivation has done so much in [55] furnishing us with specimens of various seasons, that it is no uncommon thing to meet with a rose in spring that we should take for

"The last rose of summer."

In the florists' windows, in winter (I mean in Covent Garden), we may perceive such perfections of nature that our imagination might be tempted to suppose that the summer sun could alone have produced them.

I would recommend the early spring flowers to be arranged in flower pots or in wicker baskets. In mixed groups, as a certain guide to those who do not like to trust to their own taste for blending colours, I would place lavender near pink; blue to red; white should approximate to scarlet, and yellow to purple. The small flowers particularly essential in separating the larger ones are white and yellow jasmine, nemophila cineraria, verbenas, myrtle, honeysuckle, etc., etc. The pendent flowers give great ease and elegance to a bouquet, and should be placed in first. The neck of the vase should be well filled with dried moss, which can be procured at the herbalists. Alabaster and glass vases are best adapted for the reception of wax bouquets, except when they are intended for the centre of a table, and then I prefer baskets of alabaster, wicker, or gilt; glass shades are requisite to cover either. All, or any of the last-named articles, I shall be happy to furnish to those who may kindly think proper to favour me with orders, addressed to my residence, 35, Rathbone Place.

WAX FLOWERS, AS ORNAMENTS FOR THE HAIR,

Have become so generally worn at Her Majesty's balls and drawing-rooms, that I deem it expedient to give some particular [56] instructions respecting them, so as to insure their durability and prevent their adhesion to the hair.

For the first point named, I attach a fine white wire half way up the back of each petal; this materially strengthens the flower. All white flowers should be sprinkled with my prepared arrowroot, this prevents the edges of the petals clinging to the hair, and is a protection against heat. In coloured flowers, the paint has the same effect. The stems are to be covered with narrow ribbon, green or brown (China ribbon). When the flowers are to be perfumed, the perfume is to be placed upon the ribbon.

INSTRUCTIONS FOR MODELLING FOLIAGE.

There are various ways of modelling leaves, but I would recommend them to be made of sheet wax as much as possible. Take three sheets of green wax, matching in colour the leaf you are about to imitate. It is not material whether the middle sheet is the same colour as the upper or under sheet. Cover a wire,—the size must be chosen according to the proportion of the leaf,—place the said wire when covered under one sheet—cut the wax into the form of the leaf required. Plunge the real leaf into cold water, and the wax into hot; while in a softened state press it firmly and quickly upon the wrong side of the real leaf. This will give a truthful imitation. If a real leaf cannot be obtained of any particular flower, they can be modelled from a plaister mould, which I shall be happy to furnish.

Another method is to melt a small quantity of green wax into a liquid state. With a broad flat brush wash over the wrong side of a real leaf, previously oiled with the best salad oil. [57]

The latter method may be also adopted upon a mould, soaked in warm water ten minutes previous to its being used.

The stalk must be attached afterwards, and a second layer of wax placed over.

THE VICTORIA REGIA.

"There is a splendour in the living flower."

Cut the petals from my peculiarly prepared wax; attach a wire half way up each at the back; colour the first sixteen petals with pale lemon. The remaining petals require a faint glow of pink laid on from the base towards the centre. They must be all much moulded with the large ivory curling pin, as well as assisted by the thumb and finger. The sixteen petals which constitute the two first rows, and which have been tinted pale lemon, have a deep pink vandyke or point formed at the lower end of each; round the edge of this point must be laid numerous spots and strokes of rich crimson, produced with crimson lake and minute portions of blue. Eight of the last named petals are shaded darker than the others, and are placed on first.

The centre or foundation is formed by moulding wax into a solid substance, two inches in diameter and three-quarters of an inch in depth. The stamina are very numerous, and cut according to patterns. The points are crimson, then shaded lemon, and rich pink the lower end. They are curled by passing the head of the curling pin firmly down the centre, bending the points a little back. The first four rows should fall down over the foundation, the other stand erect; by this means a direct crown is formed which contributes in a great measure to the beauty of the flower. The petals are placed on in rows of eight, with the exception of the last four, or as [58] they may be termed, sepals of the calyx. These are at the back or outside dark chocolate colour (I prepare a wax on purpose). The large green seed cup that is finally attached is cast in hot wax, and can be purchased either at my establishment, or at my counters, Soho Bazaar. The calyx and seed cup are covered with prickles: to form these, roll some shreds or strips of light green wax between the marbles moderately warm; sever them into small pieces; hold the thickest end to a lighted candle, and apply each quickly to its proper place.

In selecting this flower as the closing subject of my instructions, it may not be entirely devoid of interest to many of my pupils to be furnished with a brief detail of the derivation of its name and character, as also the place where this extraordinary production of nature was first discovered. Sir R. Schomburgk was travelling in British Guiana, in the year 1837. It was in the River Berbice he beheld it, or I may say them, for numbers were floating in all their pride and glorious beauty, and at once struck him with surprise from the majesty of their form, and brilliancy of colour. This plant flowered first in England, at Chatsworth, the seat of the Duke of Devonshire, and soon after was named "Victoria," by the gracious permission of her Majesty.

Mr. Paxton has publicly stated, that his design for the Crystal Palace originated in consequence of his having planned the house in which was grown the first specimen of this gigantic plant at Chatsworth. Thus its name will be immortalized in connexion with that of the Exhibition till time immemorial. I think it may be justly denominated an emblem of strength and power.

Before I entirely leave this subject, I cannot resist alluding to the circumstance of my withdrawing works of great magnitude (and which I had purposely prepared for competition), [59] from the late great Exhibition. It is due also to the gentlemen who formed the executive committee that a true statement should be made respecting their exclusion. A rumour having been circulated that they (the gentlemen of the executive committee), refused to give me adequate space, I am anxious to repudiate such statements, and to acknowledge that some of my best patronesses previously to the opening of the Great Exhibition, and since that period, have been various members of the families of those gentlemen and the Royal commissioners. Ample space was allotted to me in the gallery, and it was considered that as other wax flowers were to be arranged there, mine would not suffer more than the rest; but the gentleman, and I believe the only person who had anything to do with the arrangement of mine, was Mr. Owen Jones. I acquit this gentleman of any invidious feeling towards me, but can only regret that he did not personally inspect my works. If he had, I feel persuaded he would have been amazed at their magnitude and the bulk of labour executed by myself unassisted. As it is, it is more than probable that I suffer in the opinion of some, to the effect that I showed some degree of "temper" or obstinacy in withdrawing them.

I am likewise anxious that it should be known that it was not the heat of the gallery entirely that intimidated me. My plates of bent glass were much larger than any in the Crystal Palace, and the groups were arranged upon thirty hundred weight of stone. The whole formed such a huge mass that it was deemed by scientific men to be impracticable to be elevated to the gallery, without jeopardising what had been produced by me by intense labour and profuse expense. The truth of this statement can be testified by an examination of the works, which may be viewed daily at my residence from ten till five o'clock (gratuitously). They have already been inspected by *fifty thousand* visitors; and as a proof that they have excited [60] some interest and much admiration, I subjoin at the end of this little volume a few extracts from the public journals.

I have but little more to add—
"Now to the world my little book go forth,
With all thy faults."
I cannot expect it will escape the criticism and censure of some; but if it meet the approbation of the discerning, and carries out my cherished, my promised views, that of instructing the uninitiated—furthering the purposes of Wax Flower Modelling—and refreshing the memories of my earliest pupils, who may for a season have neglected so charming an occupation, I shall be more than repaid for the trials and disappointments attending the various efforts I have made to satisfy all.
"Hoping the best—ready the worst to brook,
Yet seeking friendly hearts—go forth, my little book."
"As life is then so short, we should so live and labour that we may have pleasing remembrances to console and cheer us at its close; let us work earnestly and diligently, not only for our own good, but for that of our fellow creatures:—
"Oh! let us live so, that flower by flower,
Shutting in turn, may leave
A lingerer still, for the sunset hour,
A charm for the shaded eve!"
Hemans.
[61]

EXHIBITION OF
WAX FRUITS AND FLOWERS,
BY MRS. PEACHEY,
ARTISTE TO HER MAJESTY.

The following eloquent awards of the press are placed as nearly as possible in the order of their respective dates, but the dates are necessarily omitted.

Mrs. Peachey, artiste to her Majesty, has now on private view at her rooms, 35, Rathbone Place, a superb collection of works intended for the Great Exhibition. They consist principally of an enormous bouquet of flowers and a colossal vase of fruit, both of which have been executed upon a scale never previously attempted in this country. The flowers are so arranged, that they appear to stand in a basket suspended over the surface of a pool of limpid water, in which the *Victoria Regia* and other similar plants are already floating. Nothing can be more exquisite or artistic in effect than the manner in which the various flowers are grouped. The bouquet comprises specimens of almost every flower known to the botanist, from the simple honeysuckle of the cottage garden, to the rarest and most valuable exotics of the East.

Some idea of the dimensions of the two principal works may be gathered from the fact, that the shades are nearly six feet high, the largest ever blown in England, and the flowers occupied nearly a year in modelling. It was the intention of Mrs. Peachey to forward these beautiful specimens of her skill to the Great Exhibition, where a prominent place on the ground-floor was assigned to them; but it appears, that, owing to subsequent arrangements, another space, in one of the galleries, was allotted to her, and not at all adapted to such costly and fragile productions. The heat of the sun, in such an exposed situation, would have damaged the flowers irreparably; and even if this objection did not exist, it would be impossible to have the enormous shades, with their delicate contents, raised by any machinery at command into the desired position. The exhibition is one of so novel and beautiful a character, that it will well repay a visit.—*Morning Post.*
[62]

The art of making flowers in wax has been brought to a very high degree of perfection by Mrs. Peachey, Her Majesty's artiste. There is not a floral production that she cannot truthfully and delicately reproduce with her kindly material, and she has lately executed a work which we believe defies competition in the department to which it belongs. This is an enormous bouquet, containing flowers of the most intricate structure, and supported by a rock, which peers from a lake of the brightest looking glass, decorated in its turn with waxen aquatic plants. All the flowers were modelled in the first instance from white wax, and the beautiful colours are all produced by painting. The whole group is enclosed by a shade, composed of four glass plates, so curved as to meet at the top.

The work in question is to be seen in Rathbone Place, but it was the intention of Mrs. Peachey that it should be seen at the Crystal Palace. According to her statement, she was led to believe that she would be allowed a ground-floor situation, but was only allowed a place in the gallery, so exposed to the sun, that the first hot day would have performed a work precisely the reverse of her own labours. Under these circumstances she has deemed it better that her flowers should blush unseen, than that they should melt away in a halo of visibility.

Into the Crystal controversy it is not our desire to enter, but we would testify to the excellence of Mrs. Peachey's work as being perfect of its kind.—*The Times.*

We yesterday inspected a beautiful collection of wax flowers by Mrs. Peachey, artiste to Her Majesty, now on private view at 35, Rathbone Place. We have seen many specimens of the elegant art of modelling in wax, but without exaggeration we may declare that more magnificent and truthful imitations of nature it has never been our lot to witness. The centre-piece is an immense bouquet of several hundred flowers, of almost every description, and every hue, from the gorgeous scarlet cactus to the virgin-tinted snowdrop, modelled with the closest fidelity, and arranged with exquisite taste. At the foot are models of the glorious water-lily of Guyana, the recently discovered Victoria Regia, in several stages of its development, from the close shut bud with its prickly calyx to the expanded flower. Some idea of the dimensions of this giant bouquet may be formed from the fact that it stands nearly six feet in height, and that the bent plate-glass shade with which it is covered alone cost £200.

Next to this in beauty as well as size is a vast group of fruit, fifty inches in height, the shade to which is itself a curiosity, being we believe, the largest for superficial dimensions ever yet blown in England. Besides, there are a number of smaller groups of flowers and fruit, all of singular beauty. We understand that Mrs. Peachey intended this collection for exhibition at the Crystal Palace; but, owing to some miscomprehension on the part of the commission, [63] they have been reserved for private view. The place assigned to Mrs. Peachey was, we are informed, in one of the galleries, so close to the roof as to render the solar heat too dangerous for the extremely susceptible material of which these articles are composed.—*Morning Advertiser.*

Mrs. Peachey, the artiste to her Majesty, has on view at her residence, 35, Rathbone Place, some new examples of her extraordinary skill in wax painting, originally intended for the Exhibition, but not permitted to appear there in consequence of the *locale* assigned to them being at the top of the building, where, exposed to the action of the sun, they would be in peril of dissolution. The examples consist of two remarkable models—one an enormous and magnificent bouquet, consisting of hundreds of flowers of the most intricate structure and beautiful colouring, as well as the greatest diversity of character. The violet and the *Cactus grandiflora*, with the water-lily of Guiana, and the newly discovered *Victoria regia*, form part of this exquisite group.

All the flowers were modelled separately from white wax, and the colours afterwards superinduced. The bouquet stands six feet in height, and is covered with a bent glass shade. The other model is a group of fruitage, covered with a glass shade more than four feet high, and nearly three feet across, being the largest ever yet blown in England. It was manufactured from designs supplied by Mrs. Peachey herself, and cost £200. Nothing can be more picturesque or artistic than these models: full of wonderful detail which it is impossible to pursue, and implying a marvellous amount of labour and ingenuity, they lead us to regret that any misunderstanding should have led to their absence from the Crystal Palace.—*Illustrated London News.*

Ever willing to extend our protecting ægis to the weak and unsupported, we feel ourselves called upon at the present juncture to step into the arena as the defenders of several meritorious individuals whom we conceive to have met with the most unworthy treatment in regard to the exhibition, or rather the non-exhibition of their productions of art in the Crystal Palace. We have received a number of communications from artists of first-rate talent, complaining of the exercise of undue influence in official quarters, but we have been more immediately led into an investigation of the circumstances connected therewith, by a communication from Mrs. Peachey, of No. 35, Rathbone Place, Oxford Street, artiste in wax to Her Majesty. That lady's statement is nearly as follows:—that about twelve months ago, when the erection of the building in Hyde Park was spoken of, and the nature of its contents mentioned, she, feeling anxious to prove to the world that the very high and royal patronage she enjoyed was not unmerited, sent in her subscription of five guineas towards the construction of the building, and intimated her intention of sending in some specimens [64] of her own works. She was immediately assigned a most elegant site for her display on the ground floor, in the avenue near the fountain.

Nothing could be more consonant to her wishes, and she forthwith sent in her pedestals and minor portions of framework, etc. Some time since, however, on questioning this gentleman as to the certainty of her getting the desired position, she was astonished at being told she must send her articles to No. 29, *in the gallery*. This she refused to do, and the consequence has been that the Exhibition has been deprived of some of its rarest specimens of art. The reason Mrs. Peachey assigns for not sending her works to the gallery is the impracticability of their being carried up stairs without being, from their extreme fragility, seriously injured, perhaps mutilated. Even were they to be slung up by tackle, she says they would be subject to the same risk, and her two principal works, viz.—an enormous bouquet of the most exquisitely modelled flowers, and a gigantic vase of fruit, she values at no less a sum than £1000.—*Sunday Times.*

A visit to Rathbone-place, is a stepping from the ordinary exhibitions of mere art to a miniature garden, in which may be seen grouped together the beautiful flowers and fruits of every season and every clime. We shall not attempt to describe with too nice minuteness the wonderful creations of this gifted lady's hand, but freely give our impressions as they came on our inspection of these completions—these perfections of art.

To name all the blushing subjects so fairly representing the rich and wide domain of Flora, would be far less easy of accomplishment, of enumeration, than to say that queen roses—the English rose—the delicate, the beautifully clothed lily—the crimson fuchsia—the acacia, and gorgeous tulip—the Victoria Regia, in all its stages of development, bud, blossom, flower,—were as the realities of stilly life, which seemed to say, in the expressive language of flowers—"put aside from us our glassy veils, remove our crystal shrines, that we may nod kisses to the wooing zephyrs."

Pomona, too, was there. Her thousand fruits clustered under transparent concaves. Grapes that might have moved Bacchus to press them with his rosy lips—peaches, melons, shiny currants, inviting strawberries, and crowning pineapples—all worthy the pencil of a Lance—glorious as the painting of nature, mockingly tempted us to seize the fairy prizes—reminding us of an anecdote of Swift. The facetious dean, with several friends, was invited to walk the rounds, and admire the delicious fruit bending the countless trees to the earth in the orchard of an "old acquaintance," who kindly pointed out to his most admiring guests the charming sweets by which they were surrounded; but, "sour grapes to them"—asked them not to make themselves "at home," nor offered pear nor apple. This was too much for Swift, who had a happy knack of inventing scraps of poetry to suit his purposes, and thus applied [65] himself on the occasion; "I remember that my old grandmother had a saying:—

"Always take a peach
When within your reach."

Action suited to the words quickly followed. The quick arch wit of St. Patrick's put forth his hand, and his good example was followed by all the company, who each took a peach, when within his reach. Now, we must confess that we were almost tempted to essay a similar feat of onslaught on Mrs. Peachey's magic garden, but were, fortunately for all future sight-seers, withheld by the consciousness that those many rainbow liveried sweets to the eye, were not for ourselves or Coventgarden, but were the triumphs of a skilful artiste.

And are these the works that have been, which are refused a fitting place in the high field of universal, peaceful rivalry and competition in the Crystal Palace for the works *of all nations*? What! Can this be possible? Here are the works *of our own nation not there*— excluded! Surely for the credit of the Exhibition—for the honorable name of the Executive Committee, there should be enquiry. The works cannot be said to be excluded upon their merits, for they have not been inspected by the authorities. There was, nay, there is room enough in the building in Hyde Park for this peerless and costly challenge of an English woman as an artiste. England in fair competition against the world! We looked for these gems of art in the Crystal Hall—but found them only in the catalogue! We asked where they were, and the nymph Echo answered "where!" If there be any unworthy motive for this, to us, incomprehensible exclusion of native art, let such be dissipated by the breath of public opinion. But we would fain persuade ourselves that there must be some misapprehension. The works of a lady—patronized by the Queen, to be excluded from an Exhibition open to the people of all nations— we cannot comprehend it; but for the honour and fame of the nation, hope to see in their proper places, works daily visited, and admired by the aristocracies of rank, wealth, and refined taste.

Mrs. Peachey has spared neither pains nor expense, the glass flower-shade having cost her £200; she has contributed to the Exhibition, and exhibits freely. The press has noticed the emanations of her genius, and we add our testimony.—*West Kent Guardian.*

And before passing from the wax flower group, we may add an expression of our regret, that differences of some kind prevented its including the very magnificent case and bouquet which had been prepared by Mrs. Peachey, one of the artistes in wax to her Majesty. The stand itself, which, with its contents, was on private view, is externally, more elegant than any of the cases in the Exhibition, and the flowers would have yielded to none in variety or brilliancy of tint. The reputation of Mrs. Peachey, whose artistic talent is [66] of a first-rate description, would have justified the authorities in some concession, and would have enriched this department of the Exhibition with a feature of no ordinary beauty.—*Illustrated London News.*

We have inspected, at the private residence of Mrs. Peachey (in Rathbone Place, Oxford Street,) artiste in wax-work to Her Majesty, one of the most remarkable specimens of ingenuity and industry which London at present contains. This is an immense bouquet of wax flowers which that lady had prepared for the Crystal Palace, but which are not at present within its walls, for a reason to which we will presently advert. Let us first describe this really magnificent work. On four sturdy stone columns, tastefully designed, and edged with gold, is a looking-glass platform upwards of four-feet square, and representing water. From the centre of this fairy lake rises a glass column supporting a golden basket. In this is placed a bouquet some two feet high, and of proportionate girth, in which are clustered all the flowers we ever saw, and a great many which we never saw—from the humble favorites of our *Rigolettes* and *Fleur de Maries*, up to the floral aristocracy of the conservatory. There they are exquisitely reproduced in all their graces of form and colour, and arranged with the attention to contrast and general effect which bespeaks the superintending eye of the real artist. We are afraid to say how many hundred wax flowers compose this splendid bouquet; but we can safely say that, after having walked round and round it, and, as we thought, having completely examined it, the eye continually insisted on detecting some new variety, and we finally abandoned the hope of ever becoming acquainted with the whole. From the corners of the imitative waters rise various superb specimens of water plants, fresh, cool, opaque-looking, productions; and at the foot of the glass column, as if planted by accident, spring a few of our more common and very beautiful garden flowers. The whole is covered by an enormous bent glass shade, from the centre of which rises a pretty copy of Her Majesty's crown. Nothing can be more beautiful or in better taste than the object we have described. Near it is another vase, not so large, and filled with wax fruit of every kind—the bloom of the grape, the blush of the apple, the rich brown of the nut, the velvet of the apricot, the glow of the orange, and the characteristics of a hundred other fruits being represented with a tantalizing fidelity. We would have flogged the fellow who broke the Portland Vase, but we did not feel so sure, while gazing upon these admirable imitations of the most delicious fruits, that we should have been so severe upon some earnest gourmand who might dash down the vase of which we speak, in wrath that his eye and his palate had been so nobly cheated. The two vases, one of flowers, the other of fruits, are certainly the most sumptuous specimens of wax composition we ever saw.

As we have said, these works were intended by Her Majesty's artiste for the Great Exhibition. On her applying for a site, that [67] lady states that a very admirable one was assigned her upon the ground-floor of the building, near the fountains. Upon her work being complete, she was directed to place it in the gallery. This, Mrs. Peachey considered would be to jeopardise it, from the danger so fragile a production would probably sustain in being taken up stairs, and still more from the heat of the sun, to which the wax would in that situation be exposed, and which would speedily produce Icarian results destructive to the work.—*Bell's Weekly Messenger.*

Two groups of flowers and fruit most tastefully and elaborately executed in wax by Mrs. Peachey, of Rathbone Place, have, we regret to say, been withdrawn from the Crystal Palace in consequence of an inappropriate position having been assigned them by the Committee. Mrs. Peachey, who stands unrivalled in this class of ornamental art, feeling herself aggrieved by the decision of the committee, has appealed from it to the judgment of the public, and with that view has placed her works in an apartment of her residence, 35, Rathbone Place, for inspection. The taste, the labour, the time bestowed on these magnificent works, must have been very great, and we fancy the visitors to the Crystal Palace will be greater losers by their absence from that repository than even the fair artiste herself, for they are deemed by all who have seen them the finest works of the kind ever executed.—*Morning Herald.*

We have several times during the past week inspected, with much gratification a magnificent bouquet of the most rare exotics, as also a large collection of grouped fruits, modelled entirely in wax, by Mrs. Peachey, Her Majesty's artiste in ordinary in that department of feminine accomplishment, and intended by that lady for competition in "the World's Fair." We have often had occasion to witness the extraordinary skill displayed by this lady in imitating the beauties of nature from her kindly materials, but we must confess (although previously informed that the present works outvied all the previous attempts of the artiste) that we were unprepared for designs and executions so exquisitely chaste and artistic, and true in the imitation of nature. What could have induced the executive committee of the Great Exhibition to decide upon excluding works of such elaborate labour and beauty, and these the works of an English artist, of the first standing, we are totally at a loss to conjecture. We say "excluding," for it is tantamount to exclusion to tell Mrs. Peachey that she must place such volatile work in a top gallery, exposed to the heat of a July sun, or withdraw them, although she had been previously allocated space on the basement of the building. Mrs. Peachey adopted the latter alternative, feeling it detrimental to her works, not only from the objectionable position assigned her, but also from the impossibility of having her cases, which are of a large size, conveyed into the gallery, without materially injuring designs of so fragile a nature. [68]

It is to be regretted that Mrs. Peachey should be thus compelled to adopt a measure which has deprived the Exhibition of one of its rarest specimens of art, specimens which we are certain would severely test, if not outvie,—all other competitors in that department. We are glad to know, however, that the artiste's credit will not suffer from this harsh exclusion. The labour, skill, and expense she has bestowed are already duly appreciated by a discerning public, thousands of the *elite* of the aristocracy and gentry having already visited Mrs. Peachey at her residence in Rathbone-place, all of whom have expressed the most unequivocal satisfaction and delight at the beauty of the specimens, which, they allege, are far superior to any in the Exhibition. We ourselves strongly recommend our fair readers to inspect these inimitable works, feeling certain that they will continue to be pronounced the finest works of the kind ever executed.—*Observer.*

The complaints against the partiality and want of discrimination on the part of the executive committee of the Great Exhibition in the allotment of space to the would-be exhibitors are of daily and hourly recurrence. Among the grievances which are more especially injurious to the thorough development of British industry in the more delicate and refined art in feminine accomplishments, we may mention the case of Mrs. Peachey, of Rathbone-place, the "warranted" wax florist to Her Most Gracious Majesty. This lady, one of the earliest claimants for pedestal space, on the first announcement of the intended Congregation of the Industry of All Nations, we think, has been most harshly dealt by. Her first application was duly answered, and an allotment made her of space on the basement of the building near one of the fountains, and amongst the other gems of art. Subsequently, privately, she ascertained that some alteration was made with reference to her contributions; and, on application, it was intimated to her that, in consequence of "want of room," the executive had determined on transferring her cases to class 29, situated in one of the galleries. Mrs. Peachey, on inspecting the location, objected, on the just plea that wax flowers were liable to atmospheric influence from the great heat accruing from the glass roof and plate glass surrounding her flowers; and also their material and serious injury from the impracticability of moving her compositions, composed entirely of wax, up staircases without injuring her designs. The whole has resulted in the total exclusion of one of the most beautiful contributions, designed and arranged by one of our most honoured and worthy British Artists. Since Mrs. Peachey's exclusion has been known, her studio has been visited by the most aristocratic of the nobility and gentry, who have expressed the utmost indignation at her exclusion from the great competition in the World's Fair. The contributions, which occupy a small space, consist of the most rare exotic and indigenous flowers and fruits, which so closely imitate nature as nearly to deceive the spectator, and give [69] him a desire to take and taste of the luscious banquet. Altogether the cases, which occupied her twelve months in completing, are worthy of inspection, a gratification which Mrs. Peachey affords the public by throwing open her rooms for public inspection. We recommend the admirers of imitative art to inspect these beautiful and artistic gems.—*Expositor.*

A visit to Mrs. Peachey's Studio, in Rathbone-place, is like stepping into some garden of Fairy Land, where flowers of all seasons, and fruits of every clime present themselves at once to the eye in perennial bloom. The rose is there in all its varieties, the lily, the drooping fuchsia, the accasia, the gorgeous tulip, the dahlia, the Victoria Regia in all its stages of development, bud, blossom, flower. Grapes, too, that would have moved the jolly god to press them within his ruddy lips, peaches, nectarines, currants, strawberries, and crowning pine apples, in one rare trophy, worthy the study of a Lance. Our feelings at the moment recalled vividly an amusing anecdote of Swift. The facetious Dean with several friends was invited to walk the rounds and admire the fruit in the garden of an old acquaintance, who pointed out all the beauties of his orchard, without, however, asking the company to partake of any of the tempting display. This was too much for Swift, who having a happy art of inventing rhymes to suit his purposes, applied it in the following manner on the occasion; "I remember," said he, stopping under a very heavy laden bough, "that my dear old grandmother had a saying which ran thus—

"Always pluck a peach
When within your reach."

Suiting the action to the word, he quickly put forth his hand and took and ate—an example which was not lost on those who accompanied him. Now we candidly confess that we were in an unguarded moment tempted to essay a similar onslaught on Mrs. Peachey's fruits, but, fortunately for all future visitors, were withheld by the magnificent glass shades which protect these triumphs of art. And are these the works that have been—that are refused a fitting place in that great field of universal rivalry, the Crystal Palace! What! can it be possible? Here are works of our own nation not there—excluded! Surely, for the credit of the artiste, and for its own honorable name, the Executive Committee should enquire into the matter, and if there be any unworthy motive for this, to us, incomprehensible exclusion of native art, let such be at once and for ever dissipated by the breath of public opinion. There is still ample space for them in the great building; and we hope yet to see them there in their proper place. Mrs. Peachey has spared neither labor nor expense to render her works worthy of her reputation, and the continuance of that exalted patronage which she has long enjoyed in Her Gracious Majesty the Queen, and the highest among the aristocracy, and of the honor of her country. [70] We were glad to perceive, on our visit, that although excluded from their place among the nations, these exquisite works are eagerly sought after and admired by crowds of the *elite* of fashion and taste.—*Globe.*

This highly talented lady (artiste to Her Majesty) has now on private view, at her residence, 35, Rathbone-place, Oxford-street, two splendid works of art, which were intended to have been placed in the Crystal Palace, but the space allotted to her in one of the galleries, being not at all adapted to such delicate productions, Mrs. Peachey was compelled to refrain from carrying out her intention. These beautiful productions, the sole work of Mrs. Peachey, (who is self-taught,) comprise a monster bouquet of flowers, and a large vase of fruit. The former comprehends specimens of almost every flower known in this country, from the simple violet to the full-blown magnolia; whilst in the latter we have specimens of the principal English fruits, including the luscious pine apples and the unpretending currant. Both groups are most tastefully arranged, and an enormous expense has been incurred in the getting up of the stands and glass shades. We advise our readers not to omit seeing Mrs. Peachey's novel and truly beautiful works, and we predict they will be abundantly gratified by their visit to her Exhibition.—*Reading Mercury.*

Mrs. Peachey's group of wax flowers, modelled for the Glass Palace, is now on view at her house in Rathbone-place. Mrs. Peachey, it seems, refused the space assigned her by the Committee, on the ground that heat and darkness would, the one have destroyed, and the other shrouded the marvels of her skill. The bouquet (which is in a glass case, unsurpassed for chasteness and beauty of design) is on a gigantic scale, and contains among the rarest exotics the pride of the conservatory and the garden. We were as much surprised as delighted, on paying a visit during the past week at the skill which can imitate, and even rival, nature in her most attractive aspects. Conspicuous among the lilies, and other water flowers lining the base, is the Victoria Regia in its several states. The botanist and the florist will dwell delightedly on the *cricæ*, *orchids*, *cacti*, the night-flowering cereus, etc., besides numberless others more familiar to us.—*Dispatch.*

An exhibition of wax flowers, at the residence (in Rathbone-place) of Mrs. Peachey the artiste, is a perfect curiosity of its kind. Almost every variety of English flower, exquisitely coloured, is massed into an enormous bouquet, surprising alike from the largeness of the conception and the minuteness of the execution. This beautiful piece of art was prepared for the Great Exhibition, but withdrawn by Mrs. Peachey in consequence of her dissatisfaction with the place reserved for her.—*Examiner.*
[71]
We have inspected, at the private residence of Mrs. Peachey (in Rathbone-place, Oxford-street), artiste in wax work to Her Majesty, one of the most remarkable specimens of ingenuity and industry which London at present contains. This is an immense bouquet of wax flowers which that lady had prepared for the Crystal Palace, but were not within its walls, for a reason to which we will presently advert. Let us first describe this really magnificent work. On four sturdy stone columns, tastefully designed, and edged with gold, is a looking-glass platform upwards of four feet square, and representing water. From the centre of this fairy lake rises a glass column supporting a golden basket. In this is placed a bouquet some two feet high, and of proportionate girth, in which are clustered all the flowers we ever saw, and a great many which we never saw—from the humble favorites of our *Rigolettes* and *Fleur de Maries*, up to the floral aristocracy of the conservatory. There they are exquisitely reproduced in all their graces of form and colour, and arranged with the attention to contrast and gen-

eral effect which bespeaks the superintending eye of a real artiste. We are afraid to say how many hundred wax flowers compose this splendid bouquet; but we can safely say that, after having walked round and round it, and, as we thought, having completely examined it, the eye continually insisted on detecting some new variety, and we finally abandoned the hope of ever becoming acquainted with the whole. From the corners of the imitative waters rise various superb specimens of water plants, fresh, cool, opaque-looking productions; and at the foot of the glass column, as if planted by accident, spring a few of our more common and very beautiful garden flowers. The whole is covered by an enormous bent glass shade, from the centre of which rises a pretty copy of Her Majesty's crown. Nothing can be more beautiful or in better taste than the object we have described. Near it is another vase, not so large, and filled with wax fruit of every kind—the bloom of the grape, the blush of the apple, the rich brown of the nut, the velvet of the apricot, the glow of the orange, and the characteristics of a hundred other fruits being represented with a tantalizing fidelity. We would have flogged the fellow who broke the Portland Vase, but we did not feel so sure, while gazing upon these admirable imitations of the most delicious fruits, that we should have been so severe upon some earnest gourmand who might dash down the vase of which we speak, in wrath that his eye and his palate had been so nobly cheated. The two vases, one of flowers, the other of fruits, are certainly the most sumptuous specimens of wax composition we ever saw.

As we have said, these works were intended by Her Majesty's artiste for the Great Exhibition. On her applying for a site, that lady states, that a very admirable one was assigned her upon the ground-floor of the building, near the fountains. Upon her work being complete, she was directed to place it in the gallery. This Mrs. Peachey considered would be to jeopardise it, from the danger so fragile a production would probably sustain in being taken up [72] stairs, and still more from the heat of the sun, to which the wax would in that situation be exposed, and which would speedily produce Icarian results destructive to the work. We are not disposed to enter into the question in any spirit of censure. We know too well the *innumerable difficulties* with which the Executive Committee have had to contend in arranging the contents of the enormous building, to cavil at any decision they may have arrived at; but we have now had the opportunity of seeing two very beautiful works of English industry which would have been a credit to the Exhibition.—*Morning Chronicle.*

Those forms which our continental neighbours take such wondrous care in imitating in the perishable material of muslin, Mrs. Peachey, Her Majesty's artiste, of 35, Rathbone-place, endeavours to perpetuate in the more endurable materials of wax. Naturally afraid of jeopardising the work on which so much time and labour has been bestowed, Mrs. Peachey has withheld her contribution from the Great Exhibition; whether wisely or not, we are not here called upon to pronounce.

We can only bear witness to the evidently botanical fidelity of execution with which the forms and colours so lavishly spread throughout nature have been mimicked. In wax work generally, one is made painfully aware of the all-powerful presence of the forceps, but here we notice little or nothing of the kind, this is especially the case with the small blossoms, which expand their petals throughout a monster bouquet in wax.

In thus perfecting the imitative arts, however, no sense should be left unsatisfied; to the pleasure of seeing, might be super-added that of smelling. But in this further aim might be lost sight of that great object, viz., utility, which at present is one of the aims successfully attained by Mrs. Peachey.—*Daily News.*

FINIS.

W. N. Horton, Printer, London and Greenwich.

Transcriber's Note

Punctuation within the section headings, though inconsistent, remains as published. Minor typographical errors have been corrected without note, whilst more significant amendments have been listed below.

Pg. xvi. "Lilium Lancefolium" to *Lilium Lancifolium*.

Pg. xvi & 42. "Mignionette" to *Mignonette*.

Pg. xvi. "Passa Flora" to *Passiflora*.

Pg. xvi. "Tulip, Vanthols" to *Tulip, Van Thol*.

Pg. xvi. "Cheiranthus Cheri" to *Cheiranthus Cheiri*.

Pg. 13. "convolvolus" to *convolvulus*.

Pg. 58. "Sir R. Scomburgh" to *Sir R. Schomburgk*.

Spelling errors in the press extracts remain as printed, but have been noted below:

Pg. 69. "accasia" should be *acacia*.

Pg. 70. "cricæ" should be *cricœa*.